Robert Challe:
A Utopian Voice in the Early Enlightenment

José Porrúa Turanzas, S.A.
EDICIONES

Director General:
JOSÉ PORRÚA VENERO

Vice-director General:
ENRIQUE PORRÚA VENERO

Director:
CONSTANTINO GARCÍA GARVÍA

Executive Director: American Division: BRUNO M. DAMIANI

studia humanitatis

Directed by
BRUNO M. DAMIANI
The Catholic University of America

ADVISORY BOARD

JUAN BAUTISTA AVALLE-ARCE
University of North Carolina

THEODORE BEARDSLEY
The Hispanic Society of America

GIOVANNI MARIA BERTINI
Università di Torino

HEINRICH BIHLER
Universität Göttingen

HAROLD CANNON
National Endowment for the Humanities

DANTE DELLA TERZA
Harvard University

FRÉDÉRIC DELOFFRE
Université de Paris-Sorbonne

ROBERT J. DIPIETRO
University of Delaware

GIOVANNI FALLANI
Musei Vaticani

JOHN E. KELLER
University of Kentucky

RICHARD KINKADE
University of Connecticut

JUAN M. LOPE BLANCH
Universidad Nacional Autónoma de México

LELAND R. PHELPS
Duke University

MARTÍN DE RIQUER
Real Academia Española

JOSEPH SILVERMAN
University of California (Santa Cruz)

JOSEP M. SOLA-SOLE
The Catholic University of America

ROBERT CHALLE:

*A Utopian Voice
in the Early Enlightenment*

by Sister Lois Ann Russell, S.H.C.J.

 studia humanitatis

Publisher, *printer and distributor*
José Porrúa Turanzas S. A.
North American Division
1383 Kersey Lane
Potomac, Maryland 20854
U.S.A.

© Lois Ann Russell, 1979
I.S.B.N. 0-93-5568-03-4
Library of Congress Catalog Card Number 79-90039

Impreso en Los Estados Unidos
Printed in the United States of America

To my Mother and Father,
a small tribute

"Je donne ses observations à la manière de M. de Montaigne, non pour bonnes, mais pour miennes."

Robert Challe

Contents

	Introduction	1
I	A Biographical Portrait	7
II	Government FOR and BY the People	24
III	Voyages: A Study of Man	59
IV	Religion: A Tolerant Orthodoxy	81
V	Man: A Democratic View	104
VI	Woman: Love and Marriage	122
	Conclusion	144
	Bibliography	147
	Index	157

Acknowledgements

Invaluable assistance from a number of sources has facilitated the completion of this study of Robert Challe's documentary writings: the American Province of the Sisters of the Holy Child Jesus, a faculty grant, my Sister-colleagues on the Rosemont College faculty, and devoted friends of our Society. I am deeply indebted to several eminent scholars, in particular Professor Gérard Defaux, who animated my interest in Robert Challe and wisely directed my doctoral study, "Robert Challe: A View of Society"; Professor Frédéric Deloffre, who generously shared relevant materials and recent data; Professor Otis E. Fellows, whose constructive criticisms and kindly encouragement have significantly contributed to this study.

Grateful acknowledgement is hereby made to *Eighteenth-Century Life* and to *Proceedings of the Fifth Symposium on France and North America* for permission to reprint in revised form articles which appeared in those publications.

Professor Deloffre's definitive edition of the *Journal d'un voyage aux Indes* (Mercure de France, 1979) and the attribution to Challe of a significant text, *Difficultés sur la religion proposées au P. Malebranche,* events which coincided with the publication of this study, provide new and promising avenues for further research and publication.

Sister Lois Ann Russell, SHCJ
Rosemont College
February 1979

Introduction

The transition between the classical age and the era of the Enlightenment marked in French history a decline in the prestige of absolute rule and the gradual emergence of a spirit of democracy and freedom. These social modifications were intensified and highlighted by domestic unrest and widespread enthusiasm for travel and discovery. The resulting proliferation of travel journals, comparative and critical studies, and proposals for reform at home and new structures abroad attests to this public awakening.

From these social and political currents flow the writings of an active member of the bourgeoisie, a man involved with foreign trade and colonial enterprise: Robert Challe. His social criticism, based on data relevant to the institutions of late seventeenth century France, is developed through personal observation and varied experiences, gained in large measure through travel.

Although Challe's single fictional work, *Les Illustres Françoises* (1713), enjoyed several decades of popularity during the period immediately following its publication, both author and writings lapsed into obscurity toward the close of the *Ancien Régime*. While few early critics acknowledge Challe's contribution to the development of the novel,[1] twentieth century criticism, more varied and prolific, tends to analyze Challe's literary techniques and the realistic stylistic elements of his novel. Several contemporary scholars confirm Challe's influence on the writings of such eighteenth century novelists as Prévost, Marivaux and, in particular, Richardson. Others note the timely social, political and religious themes incorporated in *Les Illustres Françoises*.[2] These recent studies have

---

[1] Two early critics are especially noteworthy: Prosper Marchand, an editor of *Le Journal Littéraire de La Haye*, whose "Préface" to the 1748 edition of *Les Illustres Françoises* was reprinted in his *Dictionnaire historique, ou mémoires historiques et critiques* (La Haye: Pierre de Hondt, 1758), 1 of 2 vols., 182–86, and Jules Champfleury whose comments on Challe's use of realism merit notice: "A mon sens, c'est le premier qui ait employé la Réalité absolue dans le roman: tous les personnages sont des petits nobles et des bourgeois du temps; ils parlent la langue de leur époque, ils portent des noms de la fin du dix-septième siècle; enfin, ils donnent une peinture fidèle des moeurs d'alors." *Le Réalisme* (Paris: Michel Lévy Frères, 1857), pp. 85–86.

[2] English Showalter, Jr., affirms Challe's literary influence, assessing *Les Illustres Françoises* as "one of the most original works of the eighteenth century . . . [which] stands as the headspring of the major themes as well as techniques of eighteenth century fiction." *The Evolution of the French Novel: 1641–1782* (Princeton: Princeton University Press, 1972), pp. 212 and 261.

In his short study of *Les Illustres Françoises*, Henri Coulet writes: "Le sérieux est en effet ce qui distingue Chasles de tous les conteurs réalistes jusqu'à lui: chez Rabelais, Sorel, Scarron, Cyrano, Furetière, le réalisme est comique. . . . Aucune oeuvre réaliste jusqu'alors n'avait été aussi solidement construite, aucune n'avoit fait paraître cette vérité intéressante et étrange des caractères, cette vivacité des dialogues, cette netteté sobre et signifiante des indications d'heure, d'atmosphère, d'attitudes, cette intensité dramatique des scènes, cette utilisation des récits au développement de l'action." *Le Roman jusqu'à la Révolution* (Paris: Armand Colin, 1967), pp. 310 and 315.

A significant contribution was made in the field of Challian criticism in the 1960's by Catherine Lafarge. Her study, *Les Illustres Françaises de Robert Challes* (New Haven: Yale University, 1966), provides a thorough analysis of the seven tales and presents the literary techniques, the realistic qualities and the stylistic elements of the novel. Professor Lafarge proves that *Les Illustres Françoises* merits serious consideration in any appreciation of the eighteenth century French novel.

Further inquiry regarding the structure, characterization and techniques of narration is available in Edgar Carpenter's study, *Some Aspects of the Novelistic Techniques of Robert Challes: Les Illustres Françoises* (Madison: University of Wisconsin, 1974).

Lawrence Forno's book is the only full-length study of Challe's writings. Although he concentrates on Challe's novel, he includes a chapter on the

built upon the research of Frédéric Deloffre, who has restored Challe to his rightful place among early eighteenth century novelists.³ Challe's correspondence with the editors of *Le Journal Littéraire de La Haye*,⁴ also brought to public attention by the work of Deloffre, provides biographical data and informed commentary on current topics. The other non-fiction writings have been consistently neglected. Reflecting the tensions of the late seventeenth and the early years of the eighteenth cen-

---

Mémoires and the *Journal*. The introduction to this study delineates its focus: "The present study dwells chiefly on *Les Illustres Françoises* as the author's most important contribution to French literature, but also includes a consideration of his *Journal d'un voyage* and *Mémoires* as significant minor works." *Robert Challe: Intimations of the Enlightenment* (Rutherford: Fairleigh Dickinson University Press, 1972), p. 15.
    ³ Frédéric Deloffre, ed., *Les Illustres Françoises* (Paris: Belles Lettres, 1959), 2 vols. The "Introduction" presents Challe's life and a study of the novel; the "Appendix" describes the available editions of Challe's writings, namely: *Journal d'un voyage fait aux Indes Orientales par une escadre de six vaisseaux commandez par Mr. Du Quesne, depuis le 24 Février 1690, jusqu'au 20 Août 1691, par ordre de la Compagnie des Indes Orientales; Mémoires de Robert Challes, Ecrivain du Roi*; "Une Correspondance littéraire au début du XVIIIe siècle: Robert Challes et le *Journal Littéraire de La Haye (1713-1718)*"; *La Suite de Don Quichotte*. Deloffre includes in the "Appendix" certain legal documents which support affirmations made in his biographical presentation.
    In 1967 Deloffre made a second edition of *Les Illustres Françoises: OEuvres complètes de Robert Chasles, Les Illustres Françoises* (Paris: Belles Lettres, 1967). The contents are identical to the earlier edition.
    Numerous other studies of Challe's life and writings by Deloffre are indicated in the bibliography. Recent personal correspondence with Prof. Deloffre mentions his forthcoming eight volume publication by Mercure de France of Challe's *OEuvres complètes*.
    Future references to the above mentioned works will be made as follows: *Les Illustres Françoises: Journal: Mémoires: Correspondance; Don Quichotte*.
    The biographical presentation has been amended in accord with recent findings of Frédéric Deloffre. Suitable references are made to the "Vie de Robert Challe," *Journal d'un voyage fait aux Indes*, eds. F. Deloffre and M. Menemencioglu (Paris: Mercure de France, 1979), pp. 16–36. All other references to the *Journal* are based on the 1721 edition, the only text available at the time of this writing.
    ⁴ Frédéric Deloffre, "Une Correspondance littéraire au début du XVIIIᵉ siècle: Robert Challes et *Le Journal Littéraire de La Haye (1713-1718)*," *Annales Universitatis Saraviensis*, 1954, 144–82.

3

turies, these texts, the *Mémoires* and the *Journal*,[5] are unquestionably social commentaries which analyze the social institutions of the French nation during the period of transition between the classical age and the era of the Enlightenment. These writings, significant in their strength of expression, clarity of detail, and depth of vision, constitute the work of the common man, a seventeenth century traveler and critic, who voices, well in advance of the eighteenth century *philosophes*, an overt and vehement criticism of his society and its concomitant abuses of political power and exploitation of its citizens.

If Challe is appreciated today as an innovative and creative novelist, his status as a social philosopher or critic remains undetermined. Scholars have not yet fully explored this aspect of his writings. A few essays, bearing on his documentary writings, affirm the rectitude of his observations and the farsightedness of his recommendations relative to the establishment and maintenance of the French colonies in Acadia. Further study is required.

Although French critics have realized the importance of Challe's influence on the eighteenth century English novel, this *rapport* has not attracted the notice of specialists in English literary criticism. Therefore few studies of Challe's writings are available to readers of English. Similarly, Challe's interest in trade foundations and the establishment of French colonies in Acadia has not stimulated American research in this area. The present study, an examination, a synthesis, and an appreciation of the social views of Robert Challe, brings to the attention of the English speaking world this contribution to social criticism. While inquiry has been made relative to literary techniques, style, and the social views expressed in the novel, material is drawn principally from Challe's documentary writings. This procedure in no way precludes references

---

[5] *Un Colonial au temps de Colbert: Mémoires de Robert Challes, écrivain du roi*, ed. A. Augustin-Thierry (Paris: Plon, 1931) and *Journal d'un voyage fait aux Indes Orientales, par une escadre de six vaisseaux commandez par Mr. Du Quesne, depuis le 24 février 1690, jusqu'au 20 août 1691, par ordre de la Compagnie des Indes Orientales* (Rouen: Jean-Batiste Machuel, 1721), 3 vols.

The manuscript of the original version of the *Mémoires* is presently available in the Bibliothèque Nationale de Paris (NAF 13799).

to *Les Illustres Françoises*, which tend to broaden the perspective, amplifying and enriching the findings. Just as Challe presents his social theories in well documented accounts, he also exposes his views of society through the medium of his fictional world and its characters, their words and attitudes. The novel, a created genre, affords freedom to construct a framework for the themes, forces, and patterns which best illustrate his theses.

The editions of Challe's writings were chosen on the basis of their accuracy, completeness, and availability. All references to the *Journal* are taken from the single complete text of this three volume work, the 1721 edition. The punctuation, accentuation, spelling, and style of these passages adhere to the original. In order to capture Challe's strength of expression, no modifications have been made. Throughout this study, quotations from Challe's writings appear as published; all editorial comments which might distract the reader are deliberately excluded. The 1931 edition of the *Mémoires*, an abridged, modernized, and somewhat corrected text, is the only available publication of this document. The two well annotated texts edited by Deloffre, the *Correspondance* and *Les Illustres Françoises*, are essentially faithful to the original syntax and style. References to these texts, indicated at the end of the material quoted, are abbreviated as follows: J; M; C; IF. It is hoped that from these editorial practices Challe's utopian voice will emerge more clearly.

Chapter I
A Biographical Portrait

The three Challian texts, the *Mémoires*, the *Journal* and the fictional work, *Les Illustres Françoises*, are closely linked to the political and religious issues which dominated French society in the second half of the seventeenth century and the early years of the eighteenth. The author of these documents experienced absolute government as established and administered by Louis XIV; he witnessed the long periods of war activity and the resulting impoverishment of the French people; he was aware of the grave religious controversies which divided the nation. This is the world of Robert Challe. This is the climate in which he lived; this is the society he studied and criticized.

Challe understands society as a group of men united by common origin, customs and laws. This union implies a mutually shared responsibility. In this context he evaluates and judges the institutions which form his society. Challe's writings reveal a man loyal to his country and to the concept of kingship. A particularly succinct line from the *Journal*, "On ne perd jamais l'amour de la Patrie" (J III, 315), echoed by a fictional figure, Des Frans, in identical terms (IF II,400), confirms his patriotism. Challe's life, despite activities on distant seas and in foreign lands, clearly exemplifies his love of the homeland.

Challe is a man of action. He is an active participant in his world. Since his writings are based upon personal, first-hand experiences, a brief sketch of his life will assist an appreciation of his social views.

Today biographical data are readily available through the research and publications of Frédéric Deloffre. Therefore, in this study, a summary presentation will suffice as background. Deloffre affirms, in his recent edition of the *Journal*, that Robert Challe is the son of Jean Challe, a bourgeois from Paris and his second wife, Simone Raymond.[1] The variant spellings of "Challe" have been resolved by Deloffre, who confirms this currently used form in preference to "Chasles" or "Challes."[2] The first name "Robert" is clearly indicated by Challe himself in *Journal* references to his saint's day, which fell on April 24. On this date he writes: "C'est aujourd'hui ma Fête" (J I, 313) and, on the same date in the following year, "Les Pilotes, ni l' Aumonier n'ont point oublié ma Fête (J III, 290). These specific references are especially surprising in light of the strongly protected anonymity of the *Journal* publication and of the letters addressed to the editors of *Le Journal Littéraire de La Haye*, in which Challe, referring to

---

[1] The most recent biographical data are available in the definitive edition of the *Journal d'un voyage aux Indes*, eds. Frédéric Deloffre and M. Menemencioglu (Paris: Mercure de France, 1979).

A daughter, Clémence, born of Jean Challe's first marriage, became a religious at the Visitation convent in Compiègne in 1660. It is possible that Challe also considered an ecclesiastical vocation and received minor orders. If this supposition is true, he abandoned his vocation, turning instead to a military career ("Vie de RC," pp. 17–18 and note 18, p. 551).

A forthcoming special issue of *Revue d'Histoire Littéraire* will provide further biographical data, some of which results from the research of Jean Mesnard and Roger Francillon.

[2] In a footnote to his article "Robert Challe, Témoin de son temps en 1716," Deloffre takes a definitive position on the question of the spelling of "Challe." He writes: "Cette orthographe [Challe], que nous adopterons désormais est la seule bonne, ainsi que l'ont montré les recherches encore inédites, de Jean Mesnard, qui m'a fait l'amitié de m'en communiquer le résultat." p. 83.

himself as "L'Auteur des Illustres Françoises," refuses to reveal his identity:[3]

> Je vous demande en grace de ne vous point informer qui je suis, et si mon nom vous est connu, de quelque manière que ce puisse être, je vous supplie de ne le pas découvrir. (C 160. Letter dated January 22, 1714.)

The various editions of *Les Illustres Françoises*, those published during Challe's lifetime as well as the numerous editions in the later years of the eighteenth century, were all anonymous. Deloffre notes the success of this anonymous work:

> Ce nombre des éditions des *Illustres Françoises* au XVIIIe siècle, sans doute près d'une vingtaine, paraîtra considérable, si l'on se souvient que le livre n'a bénéficié d'aucune publicité et que le nom de son auteur est resté inconnu. (IF, Appendice, II, 562) [4]

---

[3] Letters from the editors of *Le Journal Littéraire de La Haye* to the unnamed author of *Les Illustres Françoises* were sent through the intermediary of the abbé Bignon, an ecclesiastic whose influence and contacts were widespread. Deloffre includes the following note in his edition of the *Correspondance*: "Jean Paul Bignon, né en 1662 d'une famille de robe bien connue, embrassa l'état ecclésiastique. Cela n'empêcha pas Pontchartrain de lui confier en 1696 la direction des Académies du royaume. Il devint en 1700 Directeur de la Librairie et chef de la censure, fonctions qu'il occupa jusqu'en 1714. En 1701, il était nommé conseiller d'Etat, en 1702 Directeur du *Journal des Sçavans*. Sa carrière ecclésiastique se développait parallèlement: Député aux Assemblées du Clergé de 1692 et 1695, doyen du Chapitre de Saint-Germain l'Auxerrois, un des mieux dotés de France, de 1710 à 1721, on le nomma en 1712 président du bureau des affaires ecclésiastiques. Tel était le personnage au moment où Challes se fait adresser des lettres chez lui, par l'intermédiaire de Bocheron." p. 169.

[4] During the eighteenth century, the novel was translated into English and German: *The Illustrious French Lovers; Being the True Histories of the Amours of Several French Persons of Quality. In which are contained a great Number of Excellent Examples, and rare and uncommon Accidents; Shewing the Polite Breeding and Gallantry of the Gentlemen and Ladies of the French Nation*, Written Originally in French and translated into English by Mrs. P. Aubin, (London: D Midwinter and Co., 1739), 2 vols., and *Der illustren Frantzosinnen wahrhafte Geschichten, werinnen man in sehr besondern und ganz verschiedenen Charakteren eine Grosse Anzahl seltener und aussererdentlicher Exempel von schonen Manieren und Galanterie de Personen eines und andern Geschlechts dieser Nation findet* (Frankfurt, 1728).

Challe's writings provide other essential biographical data. The *Journal* gives the date of his birth, August 17, 1659 and his baptismal day immediately following. His formative years were spent at the *Collège de la Marche*, where he acquired a strong penchant for the Greek and Roman classics and the works of many literary and philosophical writers of the sixteenth and seventeenth centuries. From the time of completing his studies until the final years of the century, Challe's life was marked by a variety of activities, adventures and hazards. As a young man, he engaged in a military career, taking part in the mid 1670's in the war against Holland. Following the treaty of Nymwegen (1678), he obtained a post as clerk in the law office of M. Monicault. His letters to *Le Journal Littéraire de La Haye* mention studies in law and the obtaining of a law degree. The death of Jean Challe in 1681 caused him profound suffering. "Une querelle que j'eus vers la fin de la même année, m'obligeant de quitter Paris, ma famille m'en chercha un prétexte honnête" (M 264). Deloffre offers two possible explanations for this departure: a family quarrel over inheritance or some misdeed or misadventure (IF, Introd., I, XV).

Through the support of his former schoolmate and lifetime friend, Seignelay, Minister of the Navy, he obtained an administrative post with the newly formed *Compagnie des pêches sédentaires de l'Acadie*. This company, founded in February 1682, was authorized to establish on the coast of Acadia a fishing post and to trade furs and merchandise with France. A few lines from the *Acte de Fondation* are of particular interest to this study:

> S.M. ayant fait examiner en son Conseil la proposition faite par les sieurs Bergier, marchand de La Rochelle, Gautier, Boucher et de Nantes, bourgeois de Paris, d'establir dans la Coste de la Cadie [sic] une pesche sédentaire, s'il plaist à S.M. leur accorder la concession des terres qui se trouveront propres le long de ladite Coste, pour faire cet établissement et la même exemption pour les marchandises et vivres qu'ils y porteront, que les habitants desdites isles françaises de l'Amérique, et qu'ils pourront négocier auxdites isles, et en

Canada, sans y pouvoir être troublez en quelque sorte et manière que ce soit, lesquelles propositions ayant esté trouvées avantageuses pour le bien du commerce, S.M. a bien voulu l'accepter. [5]

Sharing preparatory responsibilities for this Canadian expedition with M. Bergier, who headed the enterprise, Challe travelled to Amsterdam where he also attended meetings of a scholarly group, the *Société des Gens de Lettres et d'Esprit*. When preparations for the Canadian expedition were completed, Challe was charged with the task of drawing up reports and evaluations of the French trade efforts in Acadia. These reports, anonymous, secret accounts commissioned by and delivered to Seignelay, form portions of Challe's *Mémoires*, edited and amended by their author thirty years later. At the time of their composition, the value of these accounts was recognized by the French ministry; Prosper Marchand, editor of the eighteenth century *Dictionnaire Historique*, writes: "De Challes avoit aussi fait une *Relation de Son Voiage en Canada*, dressée de même, par ordre, & pour l'instruction, de Mr. de Seignelai, & dont effectivement, il a, dit-il, fait usage."[6] Challe confirms this view:

> J'ai examiné, autant que ma jeunesse et mon peu d'expérience me l'ont pu permettre, les établissements, qui ont été fondés dans la Nouvelle-France, par MM. de Champigny, Le Borgne, de Razilly, Denis et plusieurs autres et j'ai toujours été convaincu que les causes de leur peu de progrès, de leur abandon et du péril où ils sont, tous les jours, d'être anglicanisés, viennent du peu de conduite et de la négligence de ces messieurs.
>
> En 1684, j'ai fourni à ce sujet, des Mémoires à M. de Seignelay. Ces Mémoires eurent si bien son approbation, qu'il eut la bonté d'en parler au Roi, qui voulut me voir. . . .

---

[5] *Archives des Colonies*, C 11^D, vol. 1, folio 150.
[6] Marchand, p. 185.

Mes Mémoires doivent encore exister, à moins qu'on ne les ait jetés au feu, ce que je ne crois pas, puisque M. de Seignelay m'ordonna de les remettre au net et de les écrire, entre deux marges, sur du papier de même format que l'original, parce qu'il voulait les faire relier ensemble.

The text continues with a reminder of Challe's prediction that the Acadian colony, and later Québec, would be lost to the English:

> Ces Mémoires restés à M. de Seignelay, ont dû après sa mort, en 1691, passer entre les mains de M. de Pontchartrain, et après lui, dans celles de M. de Maurepas, son fils. Je les prends à témoins, si je n'ai pas écrit, que tôt ou tard, l'Acadie serait anglaise. Je n'ai, comme on voit, rien annoncé qui ne soit arrivé. J'ai prédit la même chose pour Québec, mais dans un temps plus éloigné. (M 262)

The arrival of the company in Acadia and the selection of a site suitable for the establishment of a trading post are described in Challe's *Mémoires* and correspondence with Seignelay.

> Il se formait, dans ce temps-là, une compagnie, sous le nom de Pêche sédentaire de l'Acadie. . . .
> On m'associa dans la part de M. de Chevry et je partis, en 1682, avec Bergier, chef de l'entreprise.
> Le Roi avait concédé à la compagnie quarante lieues d'étendue de terrains, sur une profondeur illimitée. Nous ne savions où nous fixer, lorsque nous arrivâmes à ces côtes, ni en quel endroit nous établir. Bergier refusa d'aller à Saint-Pierre, qui avait autrefois été habité. Il donna pour raison, qu'il fallait que la terre n'en valût rien, puisque les Jésuites et les Gascons l'avaient abandonnée, et qu'une terre était assurément maudite, quand ces sortes de gens n'y trouvaient point à paître.
> Nous allâmes donc au cap Canceaux, et nous construisîmes notre habitation, au fond d'une anse, que les sauvages nomment Chedabouctou. (M 264–65)

The series of letters and reports forwarded to Seignelay between 1683 and 1684 includes the following organizational plans for the colony at Chedabouctou:

> Et comme la Compagnie fourniroit au port Royal et autres habitations de ladite coste de l'Accadie tout ce qui pourroit leur estre necessaire. Cela feroit qu'ils ne seroient plus obligez d'avoir aucun commerce avec Baston, et que toutes leurs pelleteries et autres marchandises reviendroient à la Compagnie de Canada, des ordres de laquelle ledit sieur Bergier est porteur, Ce qui augmenteroit considerablement les droits du Roy, et ne diminuroit en rien la traitte de Tadoussac prez Québek, Messieurs de la Compagnie de Canada n'ayant encore jamais tiré aucune pelleterie de l'Accadie, lesquelles ayant toujours esté portées jusques à present à Baston.
>
> La Compagnie au moyen de l'habitation de Chedabouctou, entretiendroit un commerce reiglé aux Isles de l'Amerique, où elle porteroit du poisson, huile, bois à bastir et charbon de terre, et autres choses dont les Isles manquent.
>
> Elle seroit aussi d'une grande utilité pour l'entretien de Quebek, en ce qu'il s'y feroit un magazin, de toutes les choses de l'Amerique dont ils auroient besoin.
>
> Outre qu'on pourroit avoir des nouvelles de Quebek en tout temps, et en donner en France s'il y avoit quelque chose de pressé.
>
> Et les vaisseaux qui chargent pour Québek, et qui reviennent ordinairement à vuide, trouvant à Chedabouctou a la veuë duquel ils passent du poisson, et autres marchandises du pays prestes pour leur retour, prendroient moins du fret qu'ils ne font presentement, ce qui diminueroit le prix des marchandises a Quebek.[7]

In due course, Challe made several crossings between

---

[7] *Archives des Colonies*, C 11^D, vol. 1, folio 181.

France and Canada: an initial expedition in 1682 aboard *Le Regnard*; a second crossing as assistant to La Boulaye; a final trip in 1686. His participation in the life of the colony was active and personal; his work with the trade enterprises led him finally and unfortunately to invest his savings in furs. With respect to the fortifications of Chedabouctou and provision against attacks by the English, Challe writes:

> Le Roi nous avoit donné des Troupes, pour garder Chedabouctou, dans l'Acadie, où la Compagnie de la Pêche sédentaire, dans laquelle j'étois pour mon malheur intéressé, s'étoit fixée dans l'enfoncement du Cap de Canceau. (J I, 398)

Challe reveals the mismanagement of La Boulaye whose "attachement aux plaisirs a causé sa perte et celle de la colonie" (M 272). Taken by surprise attack in June 1687, the fort was lost to the French. Details of this seizure are dramatically and vividly recounted in the *Mémoires* and the *Journal*:

> Les Anglais envoyèrent au fort de Chedabouctou des affidés qui remarquèrent la faiblesse des fortifications.
> Instruits de tout cela par ceux qu'ils avaient envoyés, sous prétexte de traiter du prix des barques pour la pêche, ils arrivèrent devant Canceaux à l'improviste, prirent les vaisseaux qui s'y trouvaient, dont trois appartenaient à la Compagnie et arrêtèrent tout le monde. Puis, entrant dans le golfe de Chedabouctou, ils mirent deux cents hommes à terre, à trois lieues du fort, et à travers bois, sans rencontrer personne, ils vinrent se coucher, le ventre à terre, à la porte du fort. A la pointe du jour, lorsqu'on ouvrit cette porte, ils y entrèrent l'épée et le pistolet à la main.
> Je ne puis songer à cette aventure, sans ressentir à nouveau la colère et la rage, qui me saisirent, lorsque j'appris ce malheur. La perte était pour moi d'importance. Le magasin, que j'avais laissé bien garni, devint la proie des Anglais, avec les pelleteries, qui avaient été traitées pendant l'hiver et le poisson pêché au printemps. (M 272)

If Challe is enraged at this example of poor administration and this unnecessary loss of territory and resources, the memory of the catastrophe evokes a similiarly strong reaction of indignation. Years later, during the quiet hours devoted to the composition of the *Journal*, he recalls:

Tout a été abandonné par notre Compagnie; & je n'y ai pas retourné depuis, y ayant été ruiné de fond en comble. (J I, 400)

Prisoner of the English, Challe was first sent to Boston and then to London. Here he made contact with a group of exiled Frenchmen, among whom he met Saint-Evremond.[8] The example of the simple and straight-forward approach to life of this Frenchman and the support of his friendship and his financial aid were deeply appreciated by Challe, who describes him as

grand Sectateur de la tranquilité d'Epicure; véritablement honnête homme; de moeurs simples; & tenant deux Maximes, de faire du bien à tout le monde, & de ne point faire de mal à personne. Je me suis ressenti de la premiére; & c'est le moins que je lui doive, que d'en conserver de la reconnaissance. (J I, 105)

Challe returned penniless to his native France.

Through the support of Seignelay, he secured the post of *écrivain du roi*[9] (IF, Introd., I, XX) abroad *L'Ecueil*, a ship in

---

[8] Saint-Evremond (1614–1703) was exiled in England in 1661 for the remainder of his life. His crime was the composition of a letter critical of Mazarin. Saint-Evremond "est l'écrivain le plus remarquable de la petite colonie française qui s'accroît par la venue des émigrés et que visitent des voyageurs de plus en plus nombreux." Pierre Abraham and Roland Desné, *Manuel d'histoire littéraire de la France*, 3 vols. (Paris: Editions Sociales, 1966), II, 429–30.

[9] Deloffre describes this post as follows: "Les fonctions d'un écrivain consistaient, lors d'un voyage au long cours, à tenir soigneusement un registre, paraphé chaque jour par le représentant de l'Amirauté ou de la Compagnie, sur lequel il inscrivait l'état des marchandises, des provisions, des munitions ainsi que la liste des passagers, pour noter ensuite au fur et à mesure toutes les modifications à cet état primitif, entrée et sortie des marchandises et

the fleet of the *Compagnie des Indes Orientales*. The voyage to India was both lengthy and dangerous. The route, plotted around the Cape of Good Hope and across the Indian Ocean to India and Siam, required over a year and a half on the sea (February 1690 to August 1691). Inaccurate charts, threats of enemy or pirate attacks, inclement weather conditions and a variety of illnesses and diseases combined to make the months at sea hazardous and uncertain. During a layover at the Island of Martinique en route home, Challe learned of the death of his friend and protector, Seignelay. The warmth of this friendship is revealed in a passage toward the close of the *Journal*:

> La premiere Nouvelle que j'apris en arrivant au Fort Royal, fut la mort de M. de Seignelai. Que devins-je? Je ne puis encore l'exprimer. Je ne comptai pour rien l'esperance perdue de ma Fortune, que j'avois fondée sur ses bontez pour moi. Je ne regrettai que lui, & la perte que la France faisoit d'un Homme qui començoit à suivre les traces du grand Colbert, son Pére, seul & unique Ministre, qui eut véritablement connu de quelle utilité le Commerce étoit à la France. Je passe là dessus & ne pense à M. de Seignelai, que les larmes aux yeux. (J III, 362–63)

The daily shipboard happenings and the entire span of time spent at sea are described by Challe in the three-volume log, a *Journal* which includes lengthy passages of critical reflection. The year following his return from the Far East, Challe set out again as *écrivain du roi* aboard *Le Prince*. The ensuing years in the 1690's and the early 1700's were spent in Paris and in short stays in other regions of France.

All of Challe's writings throughout these years of maritime service are directly and intimately related to his assignments as an administrator of the Canadian expeditions and as

---

provisions, décès des passagers ou d'autres personnes embarquées, etc. Le registre servait encore à conserver le procès-verbal des séances du conseil. Enfin, l'écrivain recueillait les testaments. En un mot, c'était 'une sorte de notaire ou de greffier', chargé de 'faire et recevoir tous les actes qui doivent avoir le caractère d'actes publics et authentiques' " (IF, Introd., I, XX).

écrivain du roi. They were the immediate outgrowth of his activities. Biographical data reveal him as an active participant in his society; Challe supports this view by applying to himself the saying: "Age quod agis" (J II, 261). In the mid 1690's, Challe made his literary début with his *Continuation de Don Quichotte*, a work published under a pseudonym for which Challe later claims authorship of the sixth volume of the French translation:

> Mais il en a été imprimé un autre sixieme tôme chez Thomas Amaury à Lion.C'est celui-là que je réclame, il est mis sous le nom de M. de Saint-Martin. (C 171)

In 1713 he published his novel, *Les Illustres Françoises*, a work composed during his "heures perduës" (IF, Préface, I, LIX). During this same year, he began his five years of correspondence with the editors of *Le Journal Littéraire de La Haye*. Many of the letters exchanged concerned his unpublished work, *Les Tablettes chronologiques*. This text, which the members of *Le Journal Littéraire de La Haye* were hesitant to publish, is unavailable. Challe writes of this work: "Cet ouvrage est un raccourci de ce qui s'est passé depuis la naissance de Jésus-Christ jusqu'à l'année 1702" (C 159). The definitive version of the *Mémoires* was compiled in 1716, some thirty years after the original documents had been given to Seignelay. At this time, Challe made several additions to the original text.

Similarly, the notes from the 1690–1691 sea voyage to India were compiled only after a lapse of seventeen years.[10] The "Avertissement" of the 1721 edition of the *Journal* describes it as a posthumous work. This fact is substantiated by recent research which indicates that Challe was buried on January 27, 1721 in the parish of Saint-Maurice in Chartres.[11]

---

[10] "Quoi qu'il y ait plus de dix-sept ans que ce Voyage soit fait . . ." (J I, 1).
[11] Deloffre, "Vie de RC," p. 33.

Challe's insistence upon anonymity and his apparent disinterest in the publication of the *Mémoires* may add credibility to his social criticism:

> Je n'ai point fait ce préambule [*Mémoires*] dans la vue de m'attirer de vains honneurs après ma mort; j'ai méprisé la gloire d'être auteur et je la méprise encore. (M 2)

Secure in the knowledge that the *Mémoires* will not reach the public during his life-time and that his writings are, therefore, free of the constraint of censorship, he writes: "Je n'écris pas dans le dessein que ces *Mémoires* paraissent durant ma vie, rien ne doit m'empêcher de dire mon sentiment" (M 241). His study of the errors of the recent past may prevent repetition in the future; his reflections may be considered a plea for tolerance, liberty of conscience and Christian spirit. This approach to current social problems implies a commitment to progress, a belief in man's endeavors and a faith in man's ability to build the future on lessons learned from the past and present.

The *Mémoires* are critical studies. At the same time they furnish valuable indications of Challe's ability to analyze problems and to propose fitting solutions. There is a significant amount of constructive advice in the pages of this work. Frequent occurences of such phrases as: "Voici comment je m'y prendrai . . . ;" "Je suis convaincu que . . . ;" "Je pose en fait certain que . . . ;" "Il me paraît que . . ." - all establish Challe's ability and confidence to identify problems and to propose definite means of immediate remedy.

These observations and criticisms were based on fact. Fidelity to truth, a truth clearly established by personal observation or by verifiable sources, is of prime importance to Challe. Whatever anecdotes, adventures or stories he presents to his readers must be true. Concerning the *Mémoires* he writes:

> Ceux qui aiment l'Histoire pourront trouver ici beaucoup d'endroits secrets, et que je sais d'original, qui pourraient, tant en bien qu'en mal, servir d'anecdotes à l'histoire de Louis XIV, et que je puis affirmer que ce que j'en dis est également curieux et vrai. (M, Préambule, 3)

In the *Journal* his assurances of first-hand knowledge and experience are very explicit: "toujours suis-je certain que je n'écrirai rien dont je ne sois persuadé" (J I, 107). It is clear that in this context "persuadé" implies first-hand knowledge or the word of reliable sources.

> Je n'écrirai rien que je n'ai vû moi-même, ou du moins qui ne m'ait été assuré par des gens dignes de foi, & dont la fidélité ne me paroitra point suspecte; & je distinguerai ce que j'aurai vû, d'avec ce que j'aurai apris, afin qu'on puisse distinguer l'un d'avec l'autre. (J I, 13)

These qualities of accuracy and reliability are essential elements in the field of criticism. In addition, Challe's criticism is enriched by a variety of experiences: social and literary contacts, educational opportunities, reading and travel. His rapport with administrative circles and court figures was not limited to his association with Seignelay. As the child of a royal bodyguard, Challe spent his early years in the shadow of the court. Literary contact made in the course of his career encouraged his love of erudition and his enthusiasm for scholarly debate. Three literary groups are mentioned in his writings: the *Société des Gens de Lettres et d'Esprit*, a tightly-knit group in Amsterdam which discussed literary or theological topics; *Le Journal Littéraire de La Haye*, with whose editors Challe enjoyed an extended epistolary exchange, highlighted by lengthy and at times witty replies from the members who acknowledge respect and admiration for the author of the well-received *Les Illustres Françoises*; and a literary group in Lyons about which Challe writes to his editor-friend in La Haye:

> Si vous étiez d'humeur à entretenir commerce avec des gens fort éloignez, il y en a où je suis de tres sçavans. (C 171–72)

Education also played a role in the development of his ideas. Deloffre notes the classical nature of the training Challe received:

> Ce qui importe encore davantage, c'est de retenir que Chasles a subi une très forte empreinte classique, à l'époque

> où la littérature française brillait d'un vif éclat. . . . L'observation directe du coeur humain est devenue à ses yeux le trait caractéristique de la littérature moderne. (IF, Introd., I, XIV)

Challe also mentions his familiarity with the religious and theological disputes of his day. He writes of "la quantité de Libelles ou petits Livres que j'ai lus & que j'ai sur cette matiére" (J I, 115).

Several Latin writers and Fathers of the Church, as well as seventeenth century French authors, are Challe's daily companions, especially at those moments when he finds himself aboard ship, far from the ordinary distractions and occupations of life:

> La Navire ne branle point du tout: on joue aux Cartes, aux Dames & aux Echets; on lit, & on écrit avec autant de tranquilité que dans une chambre. Pour moi, qui n'aime point le jeu, Monsieur Hurtain, & Monsieur de la Chassée, me viennent tenir compagnie de tems en tems. Du reste, St. Augustin, St. Bernard, à Kempis, m'entretiennent sérieusement; ou je me divertis avec Patrone, Ovide, Horace, Juvenal, Corneille, Racine, Moliere, ou d'autres qui ne me laissent pas seul. (J I, 90–91)

Throughout the *Journal* Challe makes frequent allusions to the works of St. Bernard or to the writings of St. Augustine in reference to man's free will, a topic much discussed by the society of his time. Challe also draws upon the classical writings of the seventeenth century to illustrate his belief in man's freedom of choice.

Challe's extensive travel experiences also added a valuable dimension to his qualities as critic. Contact with widely differing cultures and civilizations strengthened his ability to judge with open-mindedness and tolerance and provided a background against which he could better judge his own society. Challe's social criticism, clear and straightforward, reveals, in the words of a modern critic, "un peintre clairvoyant et sans doute averti de son siècle" and presents a "tableau d'autant plus instructif que ce témoin semble avoir eu l'esprit assez indépendant."[12]

The frequency and extent of his voyages can be ascertained through the *Journal*, *Mémoires* and letters. There were at least three trips to the New World; he visited Italy as well as Spain and Portugal. The most prolonged and perhaps the most difficult journey made by Challe was the sea voyage from France to India. It forms the basis of his *Journal*, a text which furnishes many insights into the thinking and reflections of its author. This work reveals to its readers the strongly held beliefs of Challe; it serves as the focal point of his reading, his wide travels and his contacts with his contemporaries.

The actual time period covered by the *Journal* is a limited one; February 1690 to August 1691. Challe's post as *écrivain du roi* required him to keep a daily log from the departure of the fleet from Port-Louis to the arrival in Pondicherry and during the return home. He was responsible for the provisions, stores, and munitions aboard ship. Such a position offered much leisure time, permitting the composition of colorful accounts of ports visited. For example, three weeks following the sailing from Port-Louis, the fleet dropped anchor at the island of Saint-Yago. Challe carefully describes the terrain, the natives of the village and finally the principal city of the island, its government and ecclesiastical buildings, its leaders and its citizens. These pages are typical of Challe's approach to new experiences: interested, at times curious, intellectually stimulated and ready to find the advantages of another civilization. His mind is receptive to the new, eager to savor and experience the unknown.

Challe possesses the faculty of reflecting on such new experiences in the light of his own life. His close contact with the formulation of commercial and colonial policy added new dimensions to his thinking. Challe enjoyed sufficient firsthand information, as well as the necessary distance achieved

---

[12] Emile Henriot, "Les *Mémoires* de Robert Challes," *Courrier Littéraire: XVIIe Siècle*, tome 2 (Paris: Albin Michel, 1959), p. 316.

through travel and the reading of the ancient writers, to form valid judgments relative to his society. His travels to and from the New World, his maritime voyage to the Far East, his experiences in England and on the continent — all familiarized him with a diversity of ways of life.

An appreciation of these qualities and aptitudes suitable for the critic would be incomplete without some consideration of Challe's character and temperament. Prosper Marchand provides the earliest description:

> c'étoit un fort aimable Homme, gai, plaisant, enjoué, ce qu'on nomme d'ordinaire un Bon-Vivant, ... c'étoit un Homme brusque, pétulant, emporté, mordant, satirique. [13]

The anonymous editor of the 1721 edition of the *Journal* praises Challe's independent thinking, his disinterested judgments, his tolerance and his sincerity:

> Il paroit que c'étoit un Homme fort dégagé des Préjugés vulgaires; à qui les Noms n'en imposoient point; qui vouloit voir par ses propres Yeux, & ne juger que par ses Lumieres; en un mot, assez desintéressé pour rendre le plus souvent justice à toutes les Nations, & même à toutes les Communions, si l'on en excepte les Anglais & les Réformez; contre lesquels il est quelquefois d'un peu trop mauvaise Humeur. Tout Catholique-Romain qu'il étoit, il ne pouvoit souffrir la Persécution: il vouloit qu'on laissât à chacun la Liberté de suivre les Lumieres de sa Conscience; & ce seul Point le fera sans doute regarder avec estime par les Honnêtes-Gens. Il étoit, d'ailleurs, vrai, franc, sincere, & si naturel, qu'il ne pouvoit se gêner pour qui que ce fût: il disoit sans fâçon tout ce qui se présentoit à son Esprit; &, comme il le dit lui-même en plus d'un endroit de cet Ouvrage, il laissoit aller sa Plume tout comme elle le vouloit. (J, Avertissement, I)

---

[13] Marchand, p. 182.

Challe is serious about record keeping and his writings. His colleagues attest to his sense of responsibility and his accurate work. High praise is meted out by the officers aboard *L'Ecueil* for Challe's method of compiling the accounts for his detailed log of the voyage to the Far East (J I, 44–45). Additional details of Challe's appearance and character are provided by Deloffre, editor of *Les Illustres Françoises*:

> Il est de taille moyenne, bien prise. Il ne porte pas de barbe, la trouvant 'un objet peu ragoûtant', sauf quand elle est très blanche. S'il aime le vin, il ne fume pas et ne mange pas de sucreries. . . . C'est un aimable compagnon, enjoué, grand causeur, toujours prêt, comme il le dit, à se laver le gosier ou à faire un bon repas. . . . Les taquineries de Chasles vont loin . . . il se déchaîne alors violemment contre ses ennemis, surtout les moines et les jésuites. (IF, Introd., I, XXIX)

The foregoing presentation of Challe's character and experiences indicates his qualities and aptitudes as a critic of his society. His views take on an added interest because of the time in which he lived and worked and the political régimes he knew. His position in the transitional period between the reign of absolutism and the more liberal era of the Enlightenment adds a further dimension to his writings. Although Challe's heritage and training are traditional and orthodox, many of the views he expresses announce the ideas and themes of eighteenth century *philosophes*. Throughout his writings, he studies and evaluates his society and its institutions; he formulates projects and offers suggestions for the achievement of his social goal, "l'utilité générale" (M 76).

Chapter II
Government FOR and BY the People

The times in which Robert Challe lived and worked, the political régimes he experienced and the social institutions he knew furnish the necessary data for his study and evaluation of contemporary society. His contribution to social criticism may be considered singular, if not unique, because of its origins, focus, and methodology. Challe's approach is marked by a combination of theoretical principle and practical application; his perspective is that of the middle-class citizen; his criticism is concerned with the welfare of the persons served by a particular form of government and not with the institutions themselves. As a political critic, he emerges as a traditional figure; he reflects seventeenth century traditions and announces beliefs and ideals to be developed more fully in the eighteenth century.

Challe's political criticism must by studied in the light of his personal conviction that in France, monarchy is a viable, positive and constructive system of government. Challe sees certain functions and services (particularly the welfare of the citizens) as inherent in good government. Absolute government, in his judgment, does not adequately fulfill these functions. The foundation of Challe's concept of government is a traditional one. He closely adheres to the teaching of St. Thomas Aquinas, whose ideas and writings command respect in the realm of Christian political thought: a monarchy is theoretically superior to other forms of government; legitimate authority is protected by God; certain limits or conditions must be incorporated into the system so that the rule of a king may not fall into the abuses which mark a tyranny; in conclusion, a royal power must be "tempered."[1] Challe follows this tradition, thereby endorsing the principle of legitimate authority in a system of government founded on Christian teaching, headed by a king whose power comes from God and whose responsibility is the welfare of his people.

Challe's concept of the moral obligations inherent in monarchical government contrasts sharply with the reality of the contemporary political situation. He envisions a mutual *engagement moral*, undertaken by both king and citizens, implying an assumption of reciprocal responsibilities and obligations. In the Christian context, the moral obligations and responsibilities of the king are rigorous and demanding; fulfillment of such obligations extends beyond the limits of the written laws of the nation. The king's authority is to be exercised with prudence and justice for the good of all his subjects; the king should frequently recall

> le serment qu'il a prêté à son sacre de rendre la justice à ses sujets et de soutenir le faible contre le fort. (M 36)

Whatever the seventeenth century controversies over royal authority and power, recognition of kingship as established and ordained by God was an acceptable principle. It was not the right to rule which evoked concern; rather, the nature of power and its interpretation.

---

[1] St. Thomas Aquinas, *On Kingship, to the King of Cyprus*, trans. Gerald B. Phelan (Toronto Pontifical Institute of Mediaeval Studies, 1949), pp. 13–24 and 34. "All power is from the Lord God," p. 34.
"Car il n'y a point d'autorité qui ne vienne de Dieu, et celles qui existent sont constituées par Dieu." St. Paul, "Epître aux Romains," 13:1, *La Sainte Bible*, traduite en français sous la direction de l'Ecole Biblique de Jérusalem (Paris: Cerf, 1961).

Louis XIV looked upon himself as an incarnation of classicist reason. All might change around him, but the king remained always the same, upholding, under God's dispensation, the immutable principles of reason and justice, a vigilant guardian of the interests of his state. Since Louis sincerely believed that he was cast for this role, he convinced most of his contemporaries that this was indeed a faithful representation of him. [2]

Divine Right implied a base of wisdom and political knowledge; therefore, power, a gift of God made directly to the ruler, should remain undivided. The problem of the concept of the royal will viewed as synonymous with national good remained unresolved.

The expression of absolutism is tempered by the fact that Louis also understood that he ruled a kingdom in which history and tradition had created a matrix of rights, customs and privileges, limiting the action of power; royal absolutism did not imply the right to arbitrary political action even in the mind of so absolute a king as Louis XIV. [3]

This same theory is described by another member of the French bourgeoisie, La Bruyère, whose writings correspond in time with some of Challe's work. Stressing the contractual nature of the relationship between a monarch and his subjects, he, too, emphasizes the responsibilities which accompany authority and power:

Il y a un commerce ou un retour de devoirs du souverain à ses sujets, et de ceux-ci au souverain. . . . Quelle heureuse place que celle qui fournit dans tous les instants l'occasion à un homme de faire du bien à tant de milliers d'hommes! [4]

---

[2] Andrew Lossky, "The Intellectual Development of Louis XIV from 1661 to 1715," in *Louis XIV and Absolutism*, ed. Ragnhild Hatton (Columbus: Ohio State University Press, 1976), p. 102.

[3] John B. Wolf, "Formation of a King," in *Louis XIV and the Craft of Kingship*, ed. John C. Rule (Columbus: Ohio State University Press, 1969), pp. 122–24.

[4] Jean de La Bruyère, *Les Caractères* in *Les Grands écrivains de la France*, ed. A. Regnier (Paris: Hachette, 1865), I, 384 and 360.

The approach of La Bruyère is a theoretical one; building on the same foundation, Challe adds a dimension of practicality by applying this principle to varying levels of human relationships: family and professional. Within the fictional family of *Les Illustres Françoises*, youthful disregard of parental wishes or injunctions can lead to tragedy. The decisions undertaken and the subsequent sufferings endured by Babet Fenoüil and Madeleine de l'Epine (fourth and fifth tales in the novel) illustrate this point. Against the wishes of a guardian in one case and parents, in the second, these young women give themselves to their lovers by a clandestine marriage or by private vow. The resulting punishments, in the form of anguish, separation, or death, demonstrate the moral to be drawn from these accounts.

In this same context, Challe finds an analogy between maritime affairs and civilian life: a seaman's rightful and necessary obedience to his captain and a citizen's obedience to his king:

La France seroit-elle montée à ce point de grandeur où elle est, si le Roi n'eut eu la fermeté de se faire obéir par tout le monde, sans distinction? Un Capitaine sur un Navire ne le

---

"Dire qu'un prince est arbitre de la vie des hommes, c'est dire seulement que les hommes par leurs crimes deviennent naturellement soumis aux lois et à la justice, dont le prince est le dépositaire: ajouter qu'il est maître absolu de tous les biens de ses sujets, sans égards, sans compte ni discussion, c'est le langage de la flatterie, c'est l'opinion d'un favori qui se dédira à l'agonie." *Ibid.*, p. 185.

The gravity of political responsibility, a major theme in Challe's writings, will be emphasized by Diderot who demonstrates that "[le] bonheur réciproque" is an essential goal of good government: "Ce n'est pas l'Etat qui appartient au prince, c'est le prince qui appartient à l'Etat; mais il appartient au prince de gouverner dans l'Etat, parce que l'Etat l'a choisi pour cela, qu'il s'est engagé vers les peuples à l'administration des affaires, et que ceux-ci de leur côté se sont engagés à lui obéir conformément aux lois." "Autorité politique," *Oeuvres complètes*, ed. J. Assézat and M. Tourneux (Paris: Garnier Frères, 1875–77), XIII, 395 and 400. In a subsequent article, Diderot stresses limited political power: "La société pour laquelle nous sommes nés nous donne des lois à suivre, des devoirs à remplir: quel que soit le rang que nous y tenions, la dépendance est toujours notre apanage, et celui qui commande à tous les autres, le souverain lui-même voit audessus de sa tête les lois dont il n'est que le premier sujet." "Indépendance," XV, 198.

représente-t-il pas? Ne doit-il pas l'imiter, suivant que sa sphere d'activité a d'étendue? (J II, 260)

Adherence to this principle of legitimate authority and acceptance of the concept of Divine Right are not equated by Challe with absolute government nor are they to be translated into an endorsement of that form of government. Challe's strongest argument concerns the concentration of power and authority in the hands of a single individual. Without some system of checks and balances, the errors and weaknesses of the absolute ruler remain unchallenged. In the text of the *Mémoires*, Challe specifically presents a catalogue of such abuses and erroneous decisions which prevailed during the reign of Louis XIV.

Challe's methodology is noteworthy. He cites with great frequency pertinent data and specific real life cases relevant to his criticism. Almost every page of the *Mémoires* refers to a particular event, names the chief "characters," indicates the time and place of the episode; each event is carefully incorporated into the criticism. This approach is well suited to Challe. His writings, a reflection of his life, exemplify personal involvement and experience, initiative and knowledge gained through hard work and enterprise.

In his study of the effects of absolute government, Challe stresses the marked contrast in public esteem for the young king during the early years of his reign and during the final decades. As a young ruler Louis XIV was revered by his people as well as by those who surrounded him at court. The close of his reign was marked by a visible and almost measurable diminishment of regard for the person of the king and for his policies. Scholars agree that the successful early decades were followed by years marked by error and failure. A variety of reasons support this evaluation.[5]

Yet, if these first decades conclusively established the supremacy of central government, the latter part of the reign demonstrated both the limits of its authority and the weak-

---

[5] Lossky, pp. 102–03.

ness of its control. War and economic distress of course played their parts, but the principal source of the crown's difficulties was its own hesitancy in arriving at decisions. [6] Challes bases much of his political criticism on the contrast between these periods. He considers the final years of this reign, the years of decline, as the natural and inevitable outcome of the series of mistakes and abuses committed by a single figure empowered with absolute authority. Challe's presentation of this marked contrast begins with references to the promising qualities of the young king. The opening pages of the *Mémoires* describe the king as follows:

> Il était né parfaitement honnête homme et on peut dire que naturellement il avait beaucoup de probité. (M 4)

He further notes an essential quality for a great leader: "Une âme toute grande et toute héroïque" (M 7). Other writers support this view and draw similar contrasts between the two extremes of the king's reign: early years marked by grandeur, esteem, awe; closing years in which adverse public opinion and criticism were audibly and bitterly expressed. As a memorialist of this reign, Saint-Simon presents personal political views through a series of court portraits. He insists that the fundamental order and foundation of the French nation are threatened by uncontrolled centralization of authority.[7] He also includes in his criticism references to the early years, highlighting the majesty and grandeur which surrounded the person of the king and his court:

---

[6] Lionel Rothkrug, *Opposition to Louis XIV: The Political and Social Origins of the French Enlightenment* (Princeton: Princeton University Press, 1965), VII.

[7] Jean-Pierre Brancourt, *Le Duc de Saint-Simon et la monarchie* (Paris: Cujas, 1971), p. 24.

The historical value of Saint-Simon's criticism is further underscored: "Les opinions de Saint-Simon sont aussi celles de certains de ses contemporains les plus illustres, et l'on retrouve les thèmes qu'il a développés sous la plume d'auteurs parfois très différents.... Pour régner en maître, Mazarin a voulu anéantir toute dignité due au mérite ou à la naissance et Louis XIV a suivi la même voie."

Jamais prince ne possède l'art de régner à un si haut point ... jusqu'au moindre geste, son marcher, son port, toute sa contenance, tout mesuré, tout décent, noble, grand, majestueux, et toutefois très naturel. ... Aussi, dans les choses sérieuses, les audiences d'ambassadeurs, les cérémonies, jamais homme n'a tant imposé. ... Le respect aussi qu'apportoit sa présence en quelque lieu qu'il fût, imposoit un silence, et jusqu'à une sorte de frayeur. [8]

This awe and reverence for the person of the king were in some manner expressed by public reaction to the official royal court, Versailles, which in the 1680's became a shrine to absolute power. The letters of Mme de Sévigné contain a contemporary account of the magnificence of Versailles and of a visitor's reaction to life at the palace:

Je reviens de Versailles; j'ai vu ces beaux appartements, j'en suis charmée. Si j'avois lu cela dans quelque roman, je me ferois un château en Espagne d'en voir la vérité. Je l'ai vue et maniée; c'est un enchantement, c'est une véritable liberté, ce n'est point une illusion comme je le pensois. Tout est grand, tout est magnifique, et la musique et la danse sont dans leur perfection. Ce fut à ces deux choses que je m'attachai, et elles me firent fort bien faire ma cour, comme étant un peu de la vocation de l'un et de l'autre. Mais ce qui plaît souverainement, c'est de vivre quatre heures entières avec le souverain, être dans ses plaisirs et lui dans les nôtres: c'est assez pour contenter tout un royaume qui aime passionnément à voir son maître. [9]

---

[8] Saint-Simon, *Mémoires* (Paris: Gallimard, 1952), IV, 981–1004.
Contemporary theater also attests to esteem for the king. Lines from *Bérénice* (presented in 1670) were understood to refer directly to the king: "En quelque obscurité que le sort l'eût fait naître,/ Le monde, en le voyant, eût reconnu son maître." Jean Racine, *Théâtre complet* (Paris: Garnier Frères, 1960), acte I, sc. 5.
[9] Mme de Sévigné, *Lettres* (Paris: Gallimard, 1960), II, 926–27. This letter is dated February 9, 1683, and addressed to the Comte de Guitaut.

More than fifty years later, this view is reiterated by Voltaire, who stresses in his *Siècle de Louis XIV* the grace and regal bearing of the king:

> Le roi l'emportait sur tous ses courtisans, par la richesse de sa taille et par la beauté majestueuse de ses traits. Le son de sa voix, noble et touchant, gagnait les coeurs qu'intimidait sa présence. Il avait une démarche qui ne pouvait convenir qu'à lui et à son rang. [10]

Some of the writers in the seventeenth and eighteenth centuries, who attest to public support and admiration of the early years of the king's reign, describe the shift in public opinion which occurred in the final decades of this long reign. Former royal strengths and virtues are seen as vices; triumphs are tarnished; grandeur and glory are replaced by decadence. In the light of more recent inquiry, the final decades of this reign tend to reveal a king dedicated to and matured by his responsibilities and firmly set upon a course of action leading toward unchallengeable monarchical control. These studies somewhat modify the image of the "all powerful autocrat" as well as the "tyrant abroad or the aspirer after universal monarchy."[11] It is nevertheless true that errors in political policy were committed by Louis XIV. His involvement in matters of state and his personal review of reports, letters, and other informative documents would seemingly add to his burden of responsibility.

It should be noted that Louis XIV expanded his authority in an effort to overcome the Fronde and to secure himself

---

[10] Voltaire, *Le Siècle de Louis XIV* in *Oeuvres complètes de Voltaire*, ed. Louis Moland (Paris: Garnier Frères, 1877–82), XIV, 435.

A second passage from this work describes the intensity of public interest in court life: "Louis XIV mit dans sa cour, comme dans son règne, tant d'éclat et de magnificence, que les moindres détails de sa vie semblent intéresser la postérité, ainsi qu'ils étaient l'objet de la curiosité de toutes les cours de l'Europe et de tous les contemporains," *Ibid.*, p. 422.

[11] Ragnhild Hatton, "Louis XIV and his Fellow Monarchs," in *Louis XIV and Europe*, ed. Ragnhild Hatton (Columbus: Ohio State University Press, 1976) p. 45.

against neighboring rulers. On one side the public endorsed
and supported strong government as personal protection of
their individual rights and interests. Opposition to absolutism
was formulated and enunciated by those who felt the need for
limited royal power. Challe argues that absolute power has led
the king to commit a series of errors:

> Mais ses [the king's] plaisirs et les flatteurs lui ont fait
> commettre des fautes terribles, qui ont bien terni sa réputa-
> tion et qui ont été cause qu'il est mort avec peu de regrets de
> ses sujets, quoiqu'il en eût été l'adoration. (M 4)

Saint-Simon denounces in a similar fashion the rule of a single
leader with unlimited power:

> Les fautes, les erreurs se sont multipliées; la décadence est
> arrivée à grands pas, sans toutefois ouvrir les yeux à ce
> maître despotique si jaloux de tout faire et de tout diriger
> par lui-même. [12]

Such a political régime, in which all centers on the person of
the king, is also criticized by Fénelon, whose task it was to
educate the young dauphin for his future political rule.
Fénelon respectfully but severely criticizes absolutism. His
Lettre à Louis XIV describes the political climate under such a
régime:

> Depuis environ trente ans ... on n'a parlé de l'état ni des
> règles; on n'a parlé que du roi et de son bon plaisir. [13]

    In Challian political philosophy, the welfare of an entire
nation and its citizens depends upon the relationship between
a king and his people. Challe believes that *la bonne foi* is an
essential element in a sound political relationship. He prizes
this quality to such a high degree that he terms it "le premier et
le plus puissant lien de la société civile" (M 31). While he states
that this spirit can exist in a monarchy, he finds that a govern-

---

[12] Saint-Simon, IV, 979–80.
[13] Fénelon, *Lettre à Louis XIV* in *Oeuvres complètes* (Paris: Gauthier Frères, 1830), XXIII, 340–41. This letter was composed in 1694.

ment based on absolutism permits (or perhaps encourages) the flourishing of the weakness of the leader. In very realistic terms he accuses the king and his ministers of appropriating possessions of their people.

> Le Roi et son Conseil qui prenaient à toutes mains, tant sur le sacré que sur la profane et qui se sont figuré que le vol n'était point un crime, et que la seule manière de voler était punissable. (M 45)

Diminishment of *la bonne foi* results in the loss of esteem for and confidence in the leader of the nation. Challe unequivocally states that Louis XIV broke faith with his people by disregarding this most powerful social bond. "Il suffira de dire que le règne de Louis XIV l'a tout à fait bannie de France" (M 45). Public opinion had so shifted in the final decades of this reign that the death of the king was viewed as a political and social deliverance. Fénelon's *Lettre* à Louis XIV refers to a definitive turning of public favor: "Le peuple même (il faut tout dire), qui vous a tant aimé, qui a eu tant de confiance en vous, commence à perdre l'amitié, la confiance et même le respect."[14] A contemporary account of this public reaction is also available in the *Mémoires* of Saint-Simon:

> Tout ce qui la [the court] composoit étoit de deux sortes; les uns, en espérance de figurer, de se mêler, de s'introduire, étoient ravis de voir finir un règne sous lequel il n'y avoit rien pour eux à attendre; les autres, fatigués d'un joug pesant, toujours accablant, et des ministres bien plus que du Roi, étoient charmés de se trouver au large; tous, en général, d'être délivrés d'une gêne continuelle, et amoureux des nouveautés. [15]

---

[14] *Ibid.*, XXIII, 345.
[15] Saint-Simon, IV, 1095.
As the news of the king's passing spread outward from Versailles to the city of Paris and then through the provinces, reaction was similar. Paris, the heart of France, was: "las d'une dépendance qui avoit tout assujetti, [et] respire dans l'espoir de quelque liberté, et dans la joie de voir finir l'autorité de

Challe outlines three major areas in this absolute rule which directly resulted in a decline in royal prestige: the king's love of "la flatterie, l'adulation et l'encens" (M 8), which persuaded him to follow the ill-conceived advice of those who flattered him; the king's desire for glory, which culminated in decades of war, high taxes and grave sufferings borne by the people; the king's "dévotion ridicule" (M 4), which inspired his efforts to achieve religious unity through the Revocation of the Edict of Nantes.

Challe contends that at times the king was uninformed of certain problems which deeply affected the lives of his subjects. The apparent distance which separated Versailles from the streets of Paris or the farmlands of the provinces was considerable. Challe relates two instances in which attempts were made by members of the king's family to inform him of the miserable living conditions of the people. The king's brother

> entreprit de lui représenter la misère du peuple. Il en reçut cette réponse, digne plutôt d'un tigre, s'il pouvait parler, que d'un roi chrétien:—"Hé bien, quand il mourrait quatre ou cinq mille de ces canailles-là, qui ne sont que très inutiles sur la terre, la France en sera-t-elle moins la France? Je vous prie de ne vous point mêler de ce qui ne vous regarde pas."

The second instance cited by Challe follows immediately upon the first. The dauphin also spoke to the king concerning the poverty of his subjects. The reply is unworthy of a Christian leader:

---

tant de gens qui en abusoient. Les provinces, au désespoir de leur ruine et de leur anéantissement, respirèrent et tressaillirent de joie.... Le peuple, ruiné, accablé, désespéré, rendit grâces à Dieu, avec un éclat scandaleux, d'une délivrance dont ses plus ardents désirs ne doutoient plus." *Ibid.*

Voltaire presents a similar picture of public reaction: "Quoique la vie et la mort de Louis XIV eussent été glorieuses, il ne fut pas aussi regretté qu'il le méritait.... Nous avons vu ce même peuple qui, en 1686, avait demandé au ciel avec larmes la guérison de son roi malade, suivre son convoi funèbre avec des démonstrations bien différentes." Voltaire, *Le Siècle de Louis XIV*, XIV, 482.

"Et vous aussi," lui dit brusquement et publiquement le Roi, "êtes-vous le procureur ou l'avocat général de la canaille?" (M 194)

Challe deplores such examples of Louis XIV's aloofness from the problems of the citizens; he censures the king for the distance between court and people. The Christian leader should entirely dedicate himself, his energies, and his abilities to the welfare of his nation. Obliged to inform himself of the issues and problems affecting the lives of his subjects, he must establish policy which clearly and consistently manifests this concern.

Reliance upon the advice of the Jesuits and confidence in court fortune seekers lead to error in decision making and poor administration. Challe formulates two questions which might be asked of the king by the God in whom his royal power originates:

> Mais que répondra-t-il, si Dieu lui demande pourquoi il a ignoré ce qu'ils ont fait de mal, puisqu'une infinité de gens le lui ont représenté? Et que répondra-t-il encore, si Dieu lui demande s'il lui avait donné et confié le gouvernement du royaume pour y régner par procureurs. (M 7)

The king's practice of blindly implementing policies counseled by the Jesuits was particularly harmful to his government. In his correspondence with *Le Journal Littéraire de La Haye*, Challe describes the Jesuits as a "société formidable meme aux testes couronnées" (C 160). This group enjoyed great influence at the royal court. Challe is convinced that the king's ideals were gravely compromised by such advisors. He writes that the king

> a été absolument corrompu par ces maudites pestes de Cour, dont les souverains sont toujours environnés. . . . En effet, ce sont eux qui ont perdu la France, Louis n'ayant régné que par eux, ou plutôt eux sous son nom. . . . Certainement, c'était son plus grand vice que d'aimer la flatterie.

The Jesuits exercised an almost immeasurable power over the

king. Challe summarizes their influence in the following terms:

> A l'égard des Jésuites, qui l'ont gouverné comme ils ont voulu, et qui lui ont fait faire une infinité d'injustices, ou plutôt qui les ont faites sous son nom, on ne doit pas s'étonner que leur pouvoir ait été arbitraire sous son règne.

According to Challe, the Jesuits convinced the king of the validity of absolute power:

> Son amour-propre et sa vanité [Louis XIV] faisaient croire, par leurs inspirations [the Jesuits], que le pouvoir absolu était le plus parfait des gouvernements. (M 7–8)

Such flatterers only served to strengthen the king's determination for personal glory. This goal inaugurated a program of heavy taxation, extensive wars and inflicted suffering on the citizens. Challe illustrates this misuse of power in several ways: first, by listing the various taxes levied on the people; second, by describing in graphic terms some of the inhumane methods employed by tax collectors; third, by presenting a picture of the nation after decades of war.

The fourth chapter of the *Mémoires* opens with a listing of the taxes imposed on the people:

> Les tailles, les impôts, les entrées et toutes les maltôtes augmentées, les charges nouvellement créées, la capitation établie, le dixième levé sur tout le royaume, ont réduit la France dans un état plus triste que quarante années de guerre civile n'auraient pu faire. (M 41)

A type of bond issued on the Hotel de Ville furnished the royal treasury with badly needed funds and, in Challe's opinion, strengthened the king's power and control over the contributors:

> Ce sont ces rentes [from the Hotel de Ville] qui sont en partie cause de l'abaissement de la France. Elles ont fourni au Roi le moyen d'attacher à ses intérêts tous ceux qui lui avaient prêté de l'argent et, en même temps, le moyen de

rendre son pouvoir arbitraire et de n'avoir plus d'autre règle dans son gouvernement que sa propre volonté, contre laquelle personne n'osait se déclarer, tant il est vrai que l'intérêt personnel l'emporte sur le général. (M 18)

Control of the citizenry was further enforced through the practice of devaluation of the currency during times of tax collecting. Such a measure caused the ruin of many citizens.

On a vu de pauvres paysans, qui avaient amassé sol sur sol, pour payer leur quote-part de la taille, être obligés, par ces diminutions, de vendre jusqu'à leurs lits, pour n'être pas encore les victimes de la voracité d'une quantité de commis, d'huissiers, de sergents et d'autres canailles. (M 98)

Challe gives the details of numerous shameful financial transactions in which the king had no direct participation, but which were executed "au nom de Louis XIV" (M 42) and through his authority. Difficulty in securing revenue resulted in increased numbers of intendants who levied taxes in merciless fashion. Although the king restricted their authority in the 1660's, their jurisdiction and power grew in the decades following the Dutch War. They became judges in their role as delegates of the king.[16] These tax collectors, more than other government officials, earn the impact of Challe's criticism. He describes them as "véritables vipères qui, pour se tirer de la bassesse de leur naissance, ont rongé leur mère jusqu'aux os" (M 41). When revenues were badly needed by the state, these tax collectors imposed unbearable forms of taxation on the citizens. Those unable to pay the requisite sums found their possessions seized and sold for a fractional part of their real value.

The burden of taxation, which rose continually, seems to have been all the harder to bear since from about 1625 France entered a long period of 'mortalities': decades of

---

[16] Roland Mousnier, "The Development of Monarchical Institutions and Society in France," in *Louis XIV and Absolutism*, ed. R. Hatton (Columbus: Ohio State University Press, 1976), pp. 45–47.

dearth, famine and high grain prices, accompanied by epidemics which at times carried off as much as 30 per cent of the population in a single year.... The 'mortalities' touched off a serious social and economic crisis, for the majority of victims came from the class of producers— peasants and artisans. Towns banned fairs and markets and the exchange of goods, for fear of spreading disease; the rich fled to their country houses; smallholders were turned into paupers and beggars, wandering in their thousands; the price of land fell, and large-scale transfer of ownership took place; city governments went into debt to pay for the care of the sick and the starving. These 'mortalities' were frequent and widespread.... Their effect was cumulative. [17]

If the *Mémoires* furnish numerous references to tax collectors, illustrations of Challe's distrust of and scorn for these civil workers are equally forceful in the context of the novel. His condemnation of the system of taxation is so strong that it is clearly reflected in the fictional world he creates. He defends the wealth of Contamine senior, earned "non pas dans les partis," but rather amassed "par des voies légitimes, c'est à dire par succession" (IF I, 69).

A further illustration of Challe's contempt for tax employees is voiced by Des Frans, who may be considered the *porte-parole* of Challe. The two uncles of Des Frans were engaged in the

> Partis, où la fortune est toujours plus ample & plus advantageuse pour les richesses. Elles ne sont pas gagnées, à ce qu'on dit, fort innocemment, mais donnent toute sorte de crédit & de pouvoir dans le monde, leur faste fait pardonner leur acquêt.

Following the death of his father, Des Frans was employed in a tax office; he soon left this employ, explaining to his mother:

---

[17] Mousnier, p. 47.

quand de devrois être le plus pauvre & le plus malheureux gentil-homme de France, je ne m'abaisserois jamais à devenir le persécuteur du Peuple & des paisans.... J'avois trop de coeur & d'honneur pour prêter la main aux cruautez qu'on exerçoit contre eux sous prétexte de lever les Droits du Roi.... J'étois trop humain pour voir d'un oeil tranquile les duretez qu'ils essuyoient, & bien loin de les ruiner & de les persecuter comme on étoit obligé de le faire dans les commissions, je donnerois tout le mien pour les en délivrer.... Mon pére avoit eû raison de regarder mes oncles comme des Juifs & des usuriers, & ... je regardois leurs commis comme des valets de boureau, ou des chiens de chasse qui quêtent pour leurs maîtres.... En un mot je voyois bien que j'étois véritablement son fils, & ... je n'étois pas né non plus que lui pour devenir ni maltotier, ni partisan; ce qui ne s'accordoit point ni avec ma conscience ni avec mon honneur. (IF II, 281–83)

Throughout his writings, Challe notes the cruelty and insensitivity of these tax collectors. Their acts of flagrant social injustice and the extent of their power incite him to outbursts of righteous anger. He recounts two incidents of such extreme cruelty that he believes that "la postérité aura peine à croire" (M 43). The first incident took place at Saint-Maixent. A young, pregnant woman, recently widowed, mother of four children was unable to pay the tax (*la taille*). The collectors entered her house in order to seize her possessions. In response to the cries and complaints of the woman, one of the collectors struck her down, causing her death. Fearful of the responsibility of the death of this woman, the collectors sought to file a statement against one of the witnesses, M. de Beauregard, who had intervened in an effort to save the family's household goods. This gentleman

fut si bien mêlé, qu'il eut besoin du crédit de tous ses amis, pour n'être pas cassé, tant, sous le règne de Louis XIV, les collecteurs d'impôts étaient considérés et ménagés.

The second anecdote concerns a young mother, a member of the Paris bourgeoisie. One day she bought half the usual order of milk for her small child. When questioned by the milkmaid, she replied bitterly:

> Mais le Roi fait si bien jeûner les pères et les mères, qu'il est juste que leurs enfants se ressentent de la dureté du temps et s'il meurt de faim, il ira, lui-même, demander dans le ciel, justice de ses bourreaux. (M 43-45)

This violent reaction against examples of social injustice is reiterated in the late 1760's by Jean-Jacques Rousseau, who relives through his writings several instances of injustice and moments of anguish caused by false accusations. One such example is recounted in the early pages of *Les Confessions*. He and his young cousin were involved; the incident was "le premier sentiment de la violence et de l'injustice" which they had experienced. Rousseau describes their reaction: "Nous étouffions, et quand nos jeunes coeurs un peu soulagés pouvaient exhaler leur colère, . . . nous nous mettions tous deux à crier cent fois de toute notre force: 'Carnifex! carnifex! carnifex!' " In this same passage Rousseau further describes his lifelong attitude vis-à-vis injustice: "Quand je lis les cruautés d'un tyran féroce, les subtiles noirceurs d'un fourbe de prêtre, je partirais volontiers pour aller poignarder ces misérables, dussé-je cent fois y périr."[18]

Challe's anger and frustration when confronted by such scenes becomes thoroughly understandable in the light of government views that suggestions for tax reform were intrusions of government policy, if not threats to the system.

As late as 1707, *La Dîme Royale*, a text by Vauban outlining a system of equitable tax distribution, was considered. This tax, assessed through land holdings, salaries, and all other sources of income, was to be levied on all citizens. Vauban's working premise was justice: the main burden of taxation should not fall on those least able to bear it. The principles

---

[18] Jean-Jacques Rousseau, *Les Confessions* in *Oeuvres complètes de Jean-Jacques Rousseau*, ed. B. Gagnebin and M. Raymond (Paris: Bibliothèque de la Pléiade, 1959), I, 20.

upon which Vauban built his system are in accord with Challian thought.[19] Such examination of government policy and acknowledgement of individual rights and responsibilities, central themes of Challe's writings, will be developed some twenty years later by an eighteenth century critic and traveler, Voltaire, following his sojourn in England. On the question of equitable taxation, he writes:

> Un homme parce qu'il est noble ou parce qu'il est prêtre, n'est point ici [England] exempt de payer certaines taxes. ... Chacun donne, non selon sa qualité (ce qui est absurde), mais selon son revenu. [20]

In this context, the humanitarian responsibilities of the king should be primary. Policies and programs which directly or indirectly exploit the citizen militate against the ideal relationship of a king to his people. The civil leader assumes a role of service, a position of power to be exercised for others, never for himself. This theme, recurring with frequency throughout the Challian texts, is also expressed with vigor by Fénelon:

> Il [the king] doit être au dehors le défenseur de la patrie, en commandant les armées; et au dedans, le juge des peuples, pour les rendre bons, sages et heureux. Ce n'est point pour lui-même que les dieux l'ont fait roi: il ne l'est que pour être l'homme des peuples: c'est aux peuples qu'il doit tout son temps, tous ses soins, toute son affection; et il n'est pas digne de la royauté qu'autant qu'il s'oublie lui-même pour se sacrifier au bien public. [21]

---

[19] "Je me sens encore obligé d'honneur et de conscience de représenter à Sa Majesté qu'il m'a paru que de tout temps on n'avoit pas eu assez d'égard en France pour le menu Peuple, et qu'on en avoit fait trop peu de cas; aussi, c'est la partie la plus ruinée et la plus misérable du Royaume; c'est elle cependant qui est la plus considérable par son nombre et par les services réels et effectifs qu'elle luy rend. Car c'est elle qui porte toutes les charges, qui a toujours le plus souffert, et qui souffre encore le plus; et c'est sur elle aussi que tombe toute la diminution des hommes qui arrive dans le Royaume." *Projet d'une dîme royale, suivi de deux écrits financiers*, ed. R. Coornaert (Paris: F. Alcan, 1933), pp. 17–18.

[20] Voltaire, *Lettres philosophiques*, XXII, 109.

[21] Fénelon, *Télémaque*, XX, 79.

This theme of government service, a concept frequently stressed by

The individual citizen was indeed exploited through excessive taxation and military conscription. Wars, undertaken as a means of further enhancing and spreading royal prestige and glory, marked the entire reign of Louis XIV. Beginning in the mid 1660's with the War of Devolution against Spain, they covered a period of over thirty years, coming to a conclusion in 1713 with the Peace of Utrecht. Such war activity was expensive, costly in lives and in revenues. Much of the burden fell on the shoulders of the peasant and the workingman.

Openly opposed to wars of aggrandizement, Challe clearly and unequivocally denounces them as the direct cause of the weakening and impoverishment of his nation and its people.

Challe further develops his opposition to war in *Les Illustres Françoises*, in which he indicates the excessive risk and loss of life incurred through poor military leadership. Terny, the hero of the second tale, complains to his friend, Bernay, of a military campaign undertaken in the mid 1670's during the severe winter season:

> Nous [Terny and Bernay] aurions bien voulu y [Paris] rester quelque tems; mais le Roi ne nous consulte pas; nous eûmes ordre de partir dès la fin de janvier, tems mal propre pour faire la guerre; mais le Roi qui ne se ménageoit pas plus que le moindre volontaire, avoit insensiblement desacoutumé les troupes d'attendre la saison. (IF I, 141)

Under the ministry of Ponchartrain, who served his government for ten years as "Contrôleur Général des Finances" (1689–1699), later becoming "Secrétaire d'Etat à la Marine et à la Maison du Roi" and finally, "Chancelier" during the early years of the eighteenth century, a series of ineffectual financial policies was enacted. Challe devotes several pages of the *Mémoires* to an evaluation of those policies and measures:

Challe, will be more fully developed by Diderot: "Le gouvernement . . . n'est pas un bien particulier, mais un bien public." "Autorité politique," XIII, 394.

his assessment is a negative one. The main thrust of his criticism stems from the suffering inflicted on the people. The fact that the government and its officials are not "at the service of" the people is a grave concern (M chaps. XVIII and XXIV). Such a situation is directly opposed to the Challian concept of good government.

> Je reviens au ministère de M. de Pontchartrain, qui réduisit le peuple à une telle extrémité, qu'il fut plusieurs fois prêt à se révolter. En effet, la misère était excessive. Le pain seul valait plus qu'un ouvrier pouvait gagner, et presque tous languissaient parce que chacun se réduisit au strict nécessaire. (M 191)

Challe considers the financial situation of France during the later 1690's as a critical one. The country was "épuisé d'argent et de crédit."

> Le peuple épuisé et tout le royaume appauvri ne pouvaient plus fournir au simple nécessaire, bien loin de pouvoir contribuer au superflu, et que plus les besoins augmentaient, plus l'argent devenait rare. (M 280)

The inevitable result of such economic distress was a serious loss of life. Challe's assessment is substantiated by Goubert whose analysis of Louis XIV's government includes the following picture of the widespread misery rampant during a one year period in the early 1690's:

> La grande majorité des Francais—et nombre d'étrangers—ont été menacés, atteints ou tués par la famine. Dans un très grand nombre de localités, l'effectif annuel des morts a doublé, triplé, quadruplé, parfois pire encore. Un grand nombre de ménages ont été rompus. . . . Un examen, même superficiel, des registres paroissiaux, montre abondamment l'étendue de la catastrophe: au moins un dixième des Français au cimetière, en quelques mois. [22]

---

[22] Pierre Goubert, *Louis XIV et vingt millions de Français* (Paris: Fayard, 1966), pp. 166–67.

There is some evidence of "tendances humanitaires" manifested in the official documents and letters of government personnel in the final years of the reign of Louis XIV.[23] Nevertheless, the scope of human suffering remains verifiable.

In addition to the disasters incurred by heavy taxation, wars of aggrandizement, and severe economic problems, the king's decision to revoke the Edict of Nantes introduced serious political, social, and religious problems. This act is a further example of Louis XIV's penchant for the centralization and unification of all facets of life, including religious commitment and practice.

> Louis' understanding of religion and philosophy was painfully limited and his policy in these matters dictated by a passionate hatred of dissidence or novelty. He intended, as God's vicegerent, to extirpate heresy and error from his kingdom; the task proved beyond his powers. [24]

Following the peace of Nymwegen (1678), the nation enjoyed an era of heightened international influence which Challe qualifies as "la période de la grandeur de la France" (M 21). For the king, this was the moment to secure unity on all sides, even unity of religious belief. Therefore, the Revocation may well be considered "as much an assertion of the principle of national unity as an affirmation of the Catholic faith."[25]

A strong supporter of the rights of individual conscience, Challe makes an unequivocal condemnation of the theory of imposed religious unity. In the writings of St. Bernard, a religious leader greatly admired by Challe, is an applicable dictum: "Religio suadetur, non imponitur." If its

---

[23] Marcel Giraud, "Tendances humanitaires à la fin du règne de Louis XIV," *Revue Historique*, CCIX (1953), 217.
"Au cours des dernières années du règne de Louis XIV se produit un mouvement d'idées humanitaires . . . qui se manifeste dans la correspondance du personnel administratif; . . . il s'exprime avec éclat dans les lettres du ministre de la marine, Jérome de Pontchartrain.

[24] H. G. Judge, "Church and State under Louis XIV," *History*, XLV (1960), 231.

[25] J. P. Gooch, *Louis XV, the Monarchy in Decline* (London: Longmans, 1962), p. 8.

corollary, strength of conviction is similarly supported by Challe, those Huguenots who ostensibly embraced "conversion" are judged with scorn, for this change of allegiance assured retention of French citizenship as well as financial gain. They were

> largement récompensés de leur apostasie, je ne la nommerai jamais conversion, parce que je n'en ai jamais vu aucun véritablement converti. Les uns ont eu des charges militaires et de robe, d'autres des pensions; et d'autres ont été diversement récompensés. (M 5–6)

Furthermore, Challe condemns the Revocation of the Edict of Nantes because of its effect upon the national economy. Those Huguenots who wished to preserve their freedom of conscience and their lives were forced to flee. This "voluntary exile" adopted by thousands of Huguenots robbed the French nation of valuable talent, industry and wealth. Challe bitterly comments on this loss:

> Ce prince [the king] a encore perdu l'amour de ses sujets par la dévotion ridicule où il a été plongé les trente dernières années de sa vie. La suppression de l'édit de Nantes a commencé la perte de la France, par l'argent que ceux qui s'en sont bannis ont emporté avec eux, et par les manufactures qui faisaient une partie du commerce du royaume, que ces bannis volontaires ont porté chez nos voisins. (M 4)

Challe's view of the Revocation is undoubtedly influenced by Colbert, Secretary of the Navy in the early 1670's, the minister who had foreseen and foretold the inevitable results of such a decision. The Revocation was published two years after the death of Colbert.

> Comme il [Colbert] voyait, de son temps, que le Conseil de conscience tendait à la suppression de l'édit de Nantes, il en prévit les conséquences et se contenta de les représenter au Roi. Certainement, cet édit subsisterait encore s'il [Colbert] avait vécu. Mais son zèle pour le Roi et le royaume ne tint pas, après sa mort, contre le zèle indiscret des faux dévots qui gouvernaient Louis. (M 75)

The Revocation led to discord within the nation; it entailed a loss of French prestige abroad. Diplomatic relations with foreign powers were weakened. Protestant allies were at the least unsympathetic; adversaries were strengthened in their determination for opposition. A modern historian appraises the Revocation in the following terms: "Inutile, inefficace, la révocation troubla, divisa, appauvrit le royaume et renforça tous ses adversaires."[26]

Although Challe's analysis and criticism recognize the negative aspects of Louis XIV's government, he does not terminate his evaluation with a simple denunciation of inept leaders and ineffectual policies. The directness of his approach merits both consideration and admiration of his political thought. This appreciation of Challe's contribution to social criticism is upheld by Henriot whose endorsement seems unprejudiced and laudatory:

> Ce n'est pas parce que Robert Challes nous le [le grand siècle] peint en noir que nous faisons confiance à son témoignage. Mais le fait est à considérer d'un témoin, d'ailleurs honnête homme, qui, du vivant même du Roi Soleil, n'était pas persuadé que tout allait bien, et qui le dit tranquillement, sachant qu'on n'imprimera ses *Mémoires* qu'après lui. Dans un temps comme celui-là, d'obéissance passive et de vérité officielle, on s'étonne toujours de découvrir qu'il y avait tout de même des esprits critiques et des hommes libres capables de voir clair. C'est à nos yeux le vif intérêt de ce Robert Challes, à qui cette liberté d'esprit fait beaucoup d'honneur. [27]

Uncontestably Challe's social criticism is significantly enriched by the attention he gives to the positive aspects of government and to the presentation he makes of constructive and sound policy capable of meeting national needs. Of prime importance is his work in the area of colonization, an enterprise he envisions as a means of supporting and fostering commerce

---

[26] Goubert, p. 123.
[27] Henriot, p. 317.

and trade with the mother country and of bettering the life of the would-be colonist.

This plan originated in Challe's personal experiences in the French colonies and trading posts in the New World (1682–1687) and was based in large measure on the economic policies of Colbert.[28] There are numerous references throughout the *Mémoires* to the dedication, integrity and progressive plans of this statesman whom Challe highly esteems. A passage in the *Mémoires* refers to Colbert's economic policy as

> si louable, si belle, si chrétienne et si digne d'un ministre qui veut s'attirer l'amour des peuples et faire leur félicité. (M 74)

He strove to develop trade outside the French frontiers; he worked to expand shipbuilding in order to provide means of commercial transport.

Early in his career Colbert organized and administered trade through companies directly responsible to the king. One of these companies which proved to be a source of wealth for the nation was the *Compagnie des Indes Orientales*, the company under which Challe sailed to India. A history of this trading company, published in the eighteenth century, provides data in support of the wisdom of such enterprises:

> C'est à la sagesse et aux soins de M. Colbert que cette quatrième Compagnie dut son Etablissement. Qui ne sçait combien dans ce grand Royaume, les Sciences, les beaux

---

[28] Colbert coordinated industries, subdivided labor and introduced a factory system. Dedicated to the welfare of the French people, he was convinced that commerce and industry were capable of enriching the nation. Claude Farrère, *Jean-Baptiste Colbert* (Paris: Grasset, 1954), p. 61.

Challe indicates cogent reasons for supporting the policies of Colbert: "A l'égard du commerce, on peut assurer que jamais ministre ne s'y est plus appliqué, mais seulement par rapport à l'intérêt du Roi, à l'utilité générale et aux richesses qu'il procurait au royaume" (M 76).

Sainte-Beuve supports this evaluation of Colbert's spirit of dedication: "Dans l'âge où le tumulte des sens distrait des grandes pensées, et où les plaisirs de la jeunesse, en rassemblant sur toute notre attention, semblent borner l'univers à notre individu, Colbert s'occupait d'être utile à la société." *Causeries du Lundi* (Paris: Garnier, 1856), VII, 267.

Arts, le Commerce, la Justice, la Religion même sont redevables à ce grand Ministre, par le nombre de Fondations Royales et d'Etablissemens qu'il produisit en leur faveur. [29]

One of Colbert's chief aims and ambitions, enthusiastically shared by Challe, was the development of flourishing colonies tightly allied to the mother country. France possessed several ports in Newfoundland, territories on Hudson Bay and in Acadia, in addition to vast stretches in Louisiana and such important islands in the West Indies as Martinique, Guadeloupe and portions of St. Kitts; in South America she had a settlement in Guiana; in Africa, Madagascar and areas of Senegal; in India, Ceylon, Chandernagore, Pondicherry and Masulipatan. Challe made the acquaintance of La Salle in 1683. The latter pointed out the importance of the foundation and fortification of a colony at the mouth of the Mississippi to serve as a safeguard for communication between the French territories in Canada and in the South along the Gulf of Mexico (M 258). Reciprocal, or at times, supportive trade between France and the colonies would serve the best interests of both, offering new lands, crops, trade of fish and furs, and thereby providing occupation for Frenchmen in the homeland. The specific plans and proposals worked out by Challe for the development of the colonies were based on his own experience of the New World and on the policies of Colbert.

The combined holdings of the French in the New World gave access to the Saint Lawrence, the Mississippi and the Great Lakes. The eventual loss of these colonies was a serious blow to the economy. At the signing of the Treaty of Utrecht in 1713, which brought to a close the War of the Spanish Succession, Louis XIV was obliged to cede to England the Acadian territory, an area forming today Nova Scotia and part of the maritime province of New Brunswick. "La France ne soup-

---

[29] M. Du Fresne de Francheville, *Histoire de la Compagnie des Indes avec les titres de ses concessions et privilèges dressée sur les pièces authentiques* (Paris: De Bure, 1746), p. 22.

conne pas l'importance de la perte qu'elle a faite" (M 274). Many Frenchmen were unaware of the consequences of these losses. Challe, on the contrary, informed by his voyages and his interest in maritime and colonial enterprises, is fully cognizant of the value of these land holdings:

> Ces cessions faites par le traité d'Utrecht ne frappent point, ou frappent légèrement les Français d'Europe, parce qu'ils n'en aperçoivent pas les conséquences. Mais ceux qui, comme moi, ont été dans l'Acadie et le Canada et qui connaissent la pêche de la morue, la fertilité du terroir, l'étendue du pays, qui ont pratiqué la traite avec les sauvages et savent la facilité que les Anglais auront à nous boucher le fleuve du Saint-Laurent: ceux-là, dis-je, savent aussi qu'il aurait été plus avantageux à la France de leur céder la Normandie, la Bretagne et même l'Aquitaine, comme ils l'ont eue autrefois, que de leur céder l'Acadie, Terre-Neuve et la baie d'Hudson. (M 24)

In a letter to Seignelay, Challe describes at length this Acadian territory and hints at possible English intervention:

> L'habitation qu'a fait le sieur Bergier à Chedaboucktou proche Campseaux coste de l'Accadie se peut aysément deffendre par sa situation, ainsy que Monseigneur le pourra voir par le plan cy attaché.
>
> La terre y est tres bonne et tres fertile, et ledit sieur Bergier en a rapporté du froment, et de l'orge, qu'il y a semé le 28 may, et qu'il y a recueilli le 18 septembre de la presente année.
>
> Pres de ladite habitation il y a une petite riviere qu'on appelle la riviere aux saulmons par la quantité de ces poissons qu'on y prend.
>
> Il y a aussi proche l'habitation la riviere qui donne le nom à Chedabouctou que ledit sieur Bergier a navigué en barque jusques à quatorze ou 15 lieues en remontant, ou il a vu du long de ses bords de tres bons et de tres beaux mats de toutte sorte de grosseur et hauteur avec divers chesnes et autres bois propres à faire bordage à bastir navires et ledit

> sieur Bergier en a rapporté deux mats et du bordage de chesne qu'il a fait visitter à la Rochelle.
>
> La Moluë est fort abondante à ladite coste et la pesche en est si bonne et si advantageuze que les Anglois de Baston (*sic*) en la nouvelle Angleterre y viennent tous les jours et en font leur plus grand commerce, quoyqu'ils ne veuillent pas souffrir que nous allions en leurs costes, comme il arriva l'année derniere à un de nos bastiments poussé de la tempeste. Lequel ils voulurent arrester et degarnir, ce qu'il n'evitta qu'en leur donnant une partie de son eau de vie et de son sel.
>
> Lesdits Anglois sous pretexte de la pesche, font encore tout le commerce de tout ce qu'il y a de pelleteries en l'Accadie et riviere Saint-Jean, ce qui en diminue extremement le nombre en France et par consequent les droits du Roy. [30]

On the basis of the Treaty of Utrecht, Challe foretells the eventual loss of all territory in North America:

> Dieu veuille que je sois mauvais prophète; mais je prévois que Québec et le Canada seront bientôt anglicanisés. Voilà une partie de ce que les plénipotentiaires de France devraient prévoir, avant de signer le triste traité d'Utrecht. (M 26)

In the years following this loss of colonial enterprises, Challe draws up proposals for a solid program of colonization: the importance of this plan cannot be overly stressed. Challe writes that it is in accord with:

> mon penchant et mon goût, qui ont toujours été portés vers les nouvelles découvertes et les établissements qu'on y pouvait tenter. (M 261)

His plan for overseas colonies may well be considered the culminating point of his social theory. He pours into this proposal his reflections relative to leadership, the role of the

---

[30] *Archives des Colonies*, C 11^D, vol. 1, folio 181.

citizen, and the bonds which unite the individual with his leader and his fellowman. Challe admits that, given the circumstances of his present society, the degree of corruption in government, and the apparent lack of dedication and sacrifice on the part of government officials, the proposals he makes and the principles he endorses may be considered idealistic.

> Je sais bien que ceci [leadership in the colonies] n'est et ne sera regardé que comme une utopie, tant que nos moeurs seront aussi corrompues qu'elles sont. Aussi je ne propose cette perfection-là qu'à titre d'exemple. (M 256)

Sound leadership is one of the foundations of good society. The working out of details relative to the selection of leaders gives Challe scope for the reiteration of his political ideals. He stresses the necessity for honest and self-sacrificing leaders, men ready to work for the welfare of the group:

> Il ne faut permettre à aucun practicien, avocat, procureur, greffier et autres sangsues de s'installer dans la colonie et n'investir d'autorité, que des gens sages, d'un esprit droit, de bonnes moeurs et, si c'est possible, assez peu portés à leur intérêt personnel, pour être toujours prêts à le sacrifier à l'intérêt général, semblables en cela aux anciens Romains, dont l'intégrité et le désintéressement étaient si grands, qu'ils étaient toujours disposés à sacrifier leurs biens et leurs personnes à la République. (M 255–56)

Challe's theoretical plan is counterbalanced by a practical and detailed proposal. Aware of the social dimension, he intends that the colony be open to all men. Contrary to former state policy which freed prisoners for colonial enterprises, Challe would offer the opportunity to the impoverished but industrious members of French society, "ceux qui sont jeunes, forts, vigoureux et en état de travailler" (M 241). Topographical considerations influenced the choice of lands suitable for a colonial foundation:

> Notre établissement était à Chédabouctou, au fond d'un golfe, qui mène à Canceaux, où plusieurs navires français, qui allaient à la pêche de la morue parée, qu'on appelle à

Paris la *Merluche,* avaient leurs dégras ou plutôt leurs chafaux, pour mieux parler matelot. (M 261)

The site having been determined, the immediate needs of the colonists are to be assessed and satisfied by such measures as the distribution of lands suitable for cultivation and the supplying of tools necessary for the clearing of these lands and the planting of crops. Specific items, to be provided for each colonist, are listed: clothing for two years, grains for sowing, hens and pigs—"le tout gratis" (M 241). Challe foresees an equitable division of labor whereby the colonists group themselves according to their talents and interests for purposes of hunting, fishing, building. Further describing this cooperative effort, central to his concept of good society, Challe writes:

> Ces ouvriers se grouperont d'eux-mêmes, par pelotons de sept, huit ou dix, à leur volonté. Les uns iront à la chasse ou à la pêche, pour la chambrée, qui se procurera ainsi plus de vivres qu'il ne lui sera nécessaire. Les autres travailleront à construire des maisons et ne cesseront ce labeur, que lorsque chacun aura la sienne, avec un jardin, qui les fournira de grains, de légumes et de fruits.
>   L'esprit de société, qui réunit naturellement les hommes, les portera à bâtir ces maisons les unes près des autres. Aussi, verra-t-on en peu de temps, s'élever des hameaux, qui seront bientôt transformés en bourgs et en villages. (M 257)

This way of life, in Challian terms, is the flowering of an "esprit de société."

Challe's attention to detail, his concern with all aspects of trade and commerce are best illustrated in his own description of the resources available to the colonists in Acadia:

> J'y marquais l'utilité de l'Acadie pour la France, l'abondance des morues, la facilité de les transporter en France, en Espagne, en Italie et par toute la Méditerranée, verte ou sèche; la profusion des poissons de riviére et du gibier de terre et d'eau, la fertilité du pays, les bois convenables à la construction des vaisseaux, les havres, propres à les bâtir et à

les lancer dans l'eau; la beauté et la profondeur des ports naturels, aptes à recevoir plus de vaisseaux qu'on n'en pourrait rassembler : tels que Canceaux, La Hève, le Port-Royal, la rivière Saint-Jean et d'autres, dont je ne me souviens plus. J'indiquais le peu de fortifications qu'il y aurait à élever, puisqu'ils sont presque tous fortifiés par la nature, sans le secours de l'art. (M 262-63)

At the close of two or three years, a group of colonists will return to France, bringing with them reports of the life in the colony.

Il est assuré que leur rapport incitera un grand nombre de Français à aller peupler cette colonie et à chercher, sous un ciel plus heureux, la tranquillité et la facilité de vivre, que la fortune et la pauvreté leur dénient dans leur patrie. Il n'est pas difficile de leur donner sujet de louer ce pays, qui, de bon par lui-même deviendra meilleur encore, à mesure qu'on le défrichera. (M 256)

There is also a religious tone projected for the colony. Challe's political and ethical orientation is Christian. In the Christian context, political authority is intimately allied with service. Exercised for the betterment of man, for his temporal and eternal well-being, power should encourage development and fulfillment, not control and restraint. Christian government, founded upon the principles of integrity, justice, mercy, and charity, views the individual citizen (created in the image of God, redeemed by Christ, and destined for eternity) with respect and tolerance. A government which endorses the Christian ethic must, of necessity, envision and foster a dual ideal: the protection and betterment of man's earthly life and the preparation for eternity.

Challe's description of the role of the Church, the services to be rendered by Church representatives, and the attention due to religious worship are strongly traditional. Recalling three of the essential marks of the Church, he writes: "La base de son établissement doit être la religion catholique, apostolique et romaine." He also devotes a lengthy passage in the *Mémoires* to listing the variety of liturgical vestments and vessels required for the proper celebrations of a liturgical nature (M 252).

In accord with his distrust of religious orders, particularly the Jesuits, Challe advocates the admission of members of the secular clergy. These Church representatives are to be directed by the civil leaders of the colony; they are to devote themselves to the welfare of the colonists. The physical wellbeing of the colonists requires the ministrations of two religious orders: the *Frères de la Charité* and the *Religieuses hospitalières*.

> Le soin qu'ils prennent des malades, à la fois pour l'âme et pour le corps, est un travail rude, qui les rend fort utiles.

These members of institutions of charity are also accountable to civil leaders. Hospital administrators will be frequently changed; each administrator is to be held accountable for the work undertaken and executed during his rule:

> Qu'on change, au moins tous les trois ans, les directeurs de ces hôpitaux, et qu'en sortant de place, ils rendent un compte exact de leur régie aux corps des officiers et des communes. (M 245–46)

In the Challian scheme the individual member of the colony is of great importance. His talents and abilities are to be respected and developed; he is to be encouraged to make his individual and personal contribution to the life of the group:

> Distinguez ceux qui ont des dispositions pour un art et leur fournissez les moyens de s'y perfectionner. Faites assembler la jeunesse à certains jours, pour l'exercer aux armes. En un mot, faites tout ce qu'une politique sage, humaine et chrétienne vous inspirera. (M 242–43)

He deplores the fact that appointments are made on the basis "d'un bonnet à cornes, d'un capuchon, d'un cotillon." The individual bears the responsibility of proving himself useful to the colony. This is a society in which "le mérite, la probité personnelle donnent seuls accès aux emplois supérieurs" (M 256).

Careful study and analysis of this section of the *Mémoires* show that the colony is intended by Challe to be a type of ideal micro-society. It serves as a summation of his basic beliefs relative to good government. Although the concept of a constitutional form of government is nowhere visible in the writings of Challe, there is a strong under-current directed toward a form of limited monarchical rule. Such a political position clearly prefigures and announces convictions of eighteenth century political thinkers, such as Voltaire who treats the theme of limited political power in his *Dialogues Philosophiques*:

> Aux murs de Westminster on voit paraître ensemble
> Trois pouvoirs étonnés du noeud qui les rassemble,
> Les députés du peuple, et les grands, et le roi,
> Divisés d'intérêt, réunis par la loi. [31]

This notion of the separation of powers and popular intervention in government is further developed by Voltaire in the early 1730's:

> La nation anglaise est la seule de la terre qui soit parvenue à régler le pouvoir des rois en leur résistant, et qui, d'efforts en efforts, ait enfin établi ce gouvernement sage où le Prince, tout-puissant pour faire du bien, a les mains liées pour faire le mal, où les seigneurs sont grands sans insolence et sans vaissaux, et où le peuple partage le gouvernement sans confusion. [32]

A similar view, echoing themes of Challian thought, is expressed by another eighteenth century *philosophe*, Montesquieu, whose political text, *De l'Esprit des Lois*, establishes that the monarchical system, well suited to the French temperament, requires a balance of power.

> Il y a dans chaque Etat trois sortes de pouvoirs: la puissance législative, la puissance exécutrice des choses qui dépendent du droit des gens, et la puissance exécutrice de celles qui

---

[31] Voltaire, *L'A, B, C ou Dialogues entre A, B, C.* XXVII, 349.
[32] Voltaire, *Lettres philosophiques*, XXII, 103.

> dépendent du droit civil. . . . Lorsque dans la même personne ou dans le même corps de magistrature, la puissance législative est réunie à la puissance exécutrice, il n'y a point de liberté; parce qu'on peut craindre que le même monarque ou le même sénat ne fassent des lois tyranniques pour les exécuter tyranniquement. Il n'y a point encore de liberté si la puissance de juger n'est pas séparée de la puissance législative et de l'exécutrice. [33]

Challe's references to the "serment" sworn by the king at the hour of his coronation imply a dual commitment: first, the gravity of a king's responsibility and, secondly, his accountability to God and to his people. A king's power and authority are circumscribed by the limits of the laws of the nation. Government should be conceived as a service for the people and an institution for which the citizens are in part responsible. From such convictions flows Challe's insistence that absolute government does not best serve the interests of France. The *Mémoires* offer numerous illustrations of Challe's belief that absolute power corrupts. He writes:

> Ce pouvoir immense, qu'il [the king] s'est attribué à leur [Jesuits'] persuasion et à leur exemple, l'a jeté dans une espèce de nécessité de violer les privilèges les plus sacrés, tant de ses propres sujets que des gens d'église, de l'un et de l'autre sexe, qui ont souffert sous son règne tout ce qu'on peut souffrir sous celui d'un prince ignorant. (M 8)

The tone of this criticism, as well as the political position which fosters it, foreshadows the view of the eighteenth century political philosopher, Montesquieu:

---

[33] Montesquieu, "De la Constitution d'Angleterre," *De l'Esprit des lois* in *Oeuvres complètes*, ed. A. Masson (Paris: Nagel, 1950), I, 207–08.

While Diderot continues this trend toward a theory of limited power, he stresses the reciprocal responsibilities of king and people and the mutual contract engaging both leader and citizens. "La puissance qui vient du contentement des peuples suppose nécessairement des conditions qui en rendent l'usage légitime, utile à la société, avantageux à la république, et qui la fixent entre des limites." "Autorité politique," XIII, 392–93.

> S'il est vrai (ce que l'on a vu dans tous les temps) qu'à mesure que le pouvoir du monarque devient immense, sa sûreté diminue, corrompre ce pouvoir jusqu'à le faire changer de nature, n'est-ce pas un crime de lèse-majesté contre lui? [34]

This synthesis of Challe's political philosophy has served a dual purpose: first, to analyze the criticisms he levels against the government of Louis XIV and to place these criticisms in the perspective of the late seventeenth and early eighteenth centuries, and, second, to ascertain Challe's positive views in reference to government and his contribution to the development of the political thought of the eighteenth century.

> The French Enlightenment is in several respects a direct outgrowth of movements, led by the aristocracy and joined belatedly by merchants, which opposed the centralizing programs and economic philosophy of the King and his ministers during the second half of the seventeenth century. [35]

Challe's approach is both practical and pragmatic. He presents specific examples of political abuse: wars of aggrandizement, excessive revenue collecting, glorification of the king, misguided religious zeal. His positive statements and suggestions are equally clear and unequivocal. Sound government in France should be built upon the rule of a wise and informed leader, namely the king. The monarchy represents a covenant relationship between the king and his people; it implies mutually accepted responsibilities. As a public service, government should concern itself with the welfare of the people through fostering the interests of the private citizen and developing his aptitudes and talents. In summation, government is an institution *for* the people; in a limited sense, government should be built and maintained *by* the people. This concept of government, somewhat idealistic and utopian

---

[34] Montesquieu, "De la Corruption du principe de la monarchie," *De l'Esprit des lois*, I, 157.
[35] Rothkrug, pp. 176–77.

in tone, assuring the liberty of conscience of its citizens and the rights of the individual members of its society, places Challian political thought in a climate of tolerance and democracy little appreciated prior to the Enlightenment.

Chapter III

Voyages: A Study of Man

The French colonies in Acadia became the focal point of Challe's travels in the 1680's. The passages in the *Mémoires* which project the foundation of the ideal colonial society are the direct result of these years spent in travel and commercial enterprises in the New World.

Challe's voyages were not limited to North America. Marchand provides a detailed list of places visited and of voyages completed:

> quatre au moins en Canada, où il fut fait prisonnier par les Anglais en 1687, & de-là mené à Boston, & en Angleterre; d'autres, à Amsterdam, en 1682; en Portugal, & en Espagne, en 1683, & en 1684; en Suede & en Danemarc; en l'Archipel, à Jérusalem, & en Turquie, où il fut encore fait prisonnier; en Irlande, 1689; aux Indes Orientales, en 1690 & 1691, en qualité d'Ecrivain du Roi sur le Vaisseau *L'Ecueil*, l'un des six de l'expédition de Mr. du Quene-Guiton, de laquelle il nous a donné une relation fort étendue. [1]

---

[1] Marchand, p. 182.
In the *Journal* Challe mentions three crossings from Canada to France: "Mes trois derniers Voyages du Canada" (J I, 261).

These varied and extensive travels were linked closely to the earning of Challe's livelihood. Travel records and descriptions of places and peoples visited are to be found in those documents required by his responsibilities (representative of Seignelay in Acadia and *écrivain du roi* aboard *L'Ecueil*, a commercial vessel in the *Compagnie des Indes Orientales*[2]).

In his study of travel accounts published in the seventeenth century, Geoffroy Atkinson asserts that in principle there are two types of men who compose travel chronicles: those (like Challe) whose occupations as functionaries, sailors, businessmen, require such documentation and, secondly, the visionary (the poet), "l'homme sensible, vibrant à toutes les impressions, et prêt à découvrir le beau, l'utile, et l'inconnu dans tous les pays." In the first instance, the account emphasizes geographical and commercial data; in the second, the value of the narrative is enhanced by the ideas expressed and the personal response of the traveler to new experiences and unknown cultures.[3]

Challe's travel documents are a synthesis of these two perspectives. They fulfill their role as the prescribed reports on the French trading colonies in Canada and as the log of the sailing to India. The accuracy of Challe's *Journal* is supported by a series of inedited letters of Charmot, a missionary aboard *L'Ecueil*. These letters confirm Challe's descriptions "dans les moindres détails."[4] However, Challe's travel documents also

---

[2] In the "Introduction" to the *Mémoires* Augustin-Thierry confuses the *Compagnie des Indes Orientales* with the *Compagnie des Pêches sédentaires de l'Acadie*, IX, note 1. Deloffre mentions this error in his article, "Robert Challe: Témoin de son temps en 1716," p. 84, note 2.

[3] Geoffroy Atkinson, *Les Relations de voyages du XVIIe siècle et l'évolution des idées* (Paris: Champion, 1927), pp. 3–4.

[4] "Non seulement le témoignage de M. Charmot, quoique beaucoup plus bref que celui de Chasles, le confirme dans les moindres détails, mais encore il évoque à plusieurs reprises 'l'écrivain' du bateau, qui semble tenir une grande place à bord, et il l'évoque précisément dans les situations où Chasles dit lui-même s'être trouvé" (IF, Introd., I, XXII).

One twentieth century critic attempts to disprove the validity of Challe's documentation: H. Le Marquand describes Challe as "ce littérateur [qui] ne

reflect the interest among the French public of the seventeenth century in voyages, foreign travel, and new cultures. Challe's predilection for discovery and adventure is manifest in his attitude toward "nouvelles découvertes" (M 261). Passages from the *Journal*, for example, which describe areas visited are marked by realism of presentation and an interest in the exotic. After nearly a month at sea, during the sailing to the Far East, the first port of call was the island of Saint Yago. Challe immediately describes the terrain as viewed from the ship:

> La Terre me paroit remplie de Montagnes & de Rochers: j'irai demain & verai ce qui m'en aura paru.

The following day, as he awaits disembarkation, he writes:

> J'écris le matin, je vas à terre, & demain je dirai ce que c'est que Saint Yago, ou du moins ce qu'il m'en aura paru. (J I, 184–85)

The mid-August arrival of *L'Ecueil* at Pondicherry for a twelve day layover further illustrates Challe's anticipatory attitude; disembarkation promises time and opportunity to investigate the region and to satisfy "un esprit aussi sceptique que le mien, qui ne se repait point de vaine spéculation, & qui voudroit voir sans enigme & sans emblême tous les secrets de la Nature à découvert" (J I, 101). Several days after dropping

---

s'est jamais penché sur une carte marine." In another passage he writes: "Au vrai, il ignore tout des choses de la mer, dont il parle en terrien." "Un Faux témoin du drame de La Hougue," *Revue Historique*, 172 (1933), pp. 61 and 60.

A footnote in Deloffre's "Introduction" to *Les Illustres Françoises* further supports the validity and accuracy of Challe's *Journal*: "Dans le *Journal de Voyage aux Indes*, Chasles raconte la cérémonie d'installation du nouveau commandant et rapporte le discours prononcé par l'amiral à cette occasion. Or M. Charmot raconte le même événement et le même discours dans son Journal inédit *(Archives des Missions Etrang*ères): La comparaison des deux textes montre l'exactitude scrupuleuse du récit de Chasles, qui est seulement un peu plus détaillé et un peu plus habile que celui de M. Charmot. Ici, quoiqu'il s'agisse d'un récit fait de mémoire, Chasles résume sans doute fort bien l'argument de la harangue de l'aumônier. On en remarquera l'intérêt du point de vue historique" (IF I, XXVII, note 62). The passage in question may be found in the *Journal*, I, 320–38.

anchor in the port of Pondicherry, Challe finds the leisure to update his *Journal*:

> Nous sommes à l'ancre devant Ponticheri. L'endroit me paroit beau; mais je n'y voi point de Fort. On dit pourtant qu'il y en a un. Quand j'aurai été à terre, je dirai comme il est fait. Car, si j'ai quelque tems à moi, de quoi je ne doute point, j'en leverai le Plan, j'irai voir les Pagodes, & j'obéirai à ma curiosité, le plus qu'il me sera possible. (J II, 159–60) [5]

This eager, open-minded approach leads Challe to consider the differences among peoples. He values such differences; he delights in describing new usages and customs. For example, he composes a lengthy description of the wearing apparel of the natives of Pondicherry. His text is graphic and picturesque:

> Les habillemens des Banians sont uniformes pour la façon: il n'y a que la couleur qui differe. Je ne puis mieux les peindre, qu'ils le sont dans les Tableaux qui sont à Nôtre-Dame & ailleurs, & dans les Tapisseries où les Apôtres sont représentez. Deux grandes simares l'une sur l'autre, qui leur tombent depuis le col jusques aux piez, & qui relevent le hauteur de leur corps, sont leur habillement. Un turban fort gros & fort beau, de mousseline très fine & très blanche, avec une barbe bien longue, mais bien coupée & bien parfumée, sont l'ornement de leur tête. Un sabre large & court, dont le soureau est couvert de plaques d'or, & la poignée enrichie de diamans, par leur côté, où il est soûtenu par une grosse chaine d'or à deux endroits, à peu près comme les Housarts.

For the purpose of this study, the concluding sentence in this description is, perhaps, the most significant. Challe acknow-

---

[5] "Je n'ai point écrit depuis le 12 du courant. Parce que j'ai presque toûjours resté à terre, ou tellement occupé à bord, que je n'ai pas eu un moment à moi; mais, à présent, que nous sommes sous les voiles, je vais écrire, en un seul Article, tout ce qui me paroit de Ponticheri, ayant mes memoires tout prêts" (J II, 161). Challe devotes the next fifty-seven pages of the *Journal* to this "Article."

ledges the exotic nature of such dress. At the same time he appreciates its beauty and majesty; "Cette maniere de vêtement paroit d'abord étrange; mais, plus on s'y accoûtume, plus elle paroît majestueuse" (J III, 74–75).

In all the accounts of voyages undertaken by Frenchmen of the seventeenth century, the reader is aware of a constant comparison of distant lands with European countries. "Chaque livre de voyage est, en quelque sorte, un livre de critique. Il y a aussi la comparaison sur laquelle on attire, consciemment et volontairement, l'attention."[6] In a certain theoretical sense, Challe's travel documents recall the age-old tradition of utopian writings which demonstrate a system founded on the known and the imperfect, leading to the unknown and presumably improved or ameliorated. In the words of Albert Soboul, a twentieth century authority in the area of utopian societies, this literary tradition may be defined as follows:

> D'un monde connu et critiquable à un monde inconnu et meilleur: le procédé est le même. Et donc deux sociétés, deux systèmes confrontés et comparés. Le monde inconnu, sauvegardé par son isolement, son insularité, ... se distingue par son altérité et sert comme un miroir au monde connu du départ. La pensée utopique procède par comparaison; elle analyse le monde connu par l'intermédiaire d'un monde inconnu imaginé, radicalement différent. Il est vrai que la comparaison demeure implicite, des deux termes celui du monde inconnu réel étant sous-entendu. Etant admis que le monde inconnu est meilleur et qu'il sert de repoussoir à ce monde réel de misère et de malheur. L'utopie ne saurait être indifférente aux valeurs. [7]

Although Challe's writings indicate certain cultural comparisons (between France and the Far East or the New World), his

---

[6] Atkinson, *Les Relations de voyages*, p. 187.
[7] Irmgard Hartig and Albert Soboul. *Pour une histoire de l'utopie en France, au XVIIIe siècle* (Paris: Société des Etudes Robespierristes, 1977), p. 9.

texts, straightforward accounts of travel experiences enriched by personal reactions and reflections, distinguish themselves from such writings as the letter of the Persian travelers, Rica and Usbek in *Les Lettres Persanes* or the adventures of the giant, inhabitant of the star Sirius in *Micromégas*, whose authors, through fictional voyages, set out to initiate social, political or religious reform through criticism of contemporary systems.[8] In the case of Challe, the voyager is the author; the voyage actually takes place; the observations noted and the comparisons and judgments recorded are direct. Satire is absent. His documents reflect sincere respect for new and strange customs, institutions and usages. He views the new and the different as inherently enriching. His writings reflect an almost joyful anticipation of discovery and a sincere satisfaction with new findings. Challe does not exploit these cultural differences in order to criticize contemporary French society. His stance vis-à-vis cultural differences is essentially that of a loyal Frenchman and a member of the Church. As a voyager he assumes the role of a responsible representative of his civilization; he takes care to present his cultural heritage in a positive light; he is concerned that his homeland and his Church be respected.

In the course of his travels Challe abandons none of his strongly held convictions. He remains the humanitarian, disturbed by human suffering and angered by misguided enthusiasms. For example, his social conscience is stirred by the conditions under which the sailors live and work aboard *L'Ecueil*.

> Ils travaillent & fatiguent beaucoup nuit & jour, au hasard de leur vie: ils sont mal nouris, en comparaison de ce que les ouvriers mangent à terre; peu soignez & avec cela quelquefois bien battus!

---

[8] Michèle Duchet offers a definition of an eighteenth century concept of anthropology in the following terms: "L'emploi du mot *anthropologie* . . . lorsqu'il s'agit de Voltaire, de Rousseau, de Diderot et d'Helvétius . . . n'est qu'un moyen de fonder une morale et une politique," *Anthropologie et histoire au siècle des lumières* (Paris: Maspero, 1971), p. 19.

A prompt, unquestioning obedience is required of these sailors. Challe describes their reaction to an order to abandon their trunks in order to prepare the ship for battle:

> Afin de n'être point tant incommodé à notre premier Combat, . . . & afin que l'entre-deux-ponts soit plus libre, on a fait jetter à bas les coffres des Matelots. Il est inutile de leur prêcher l'obéissance qui s'observe dans les Couvents; elle n'est pas plus grande que celle qui s'observe à la Mer. Nos Matelots ont eux-mêmes, au premier commandement, mis la hache dans leurs coffres.

Challe concludes, as he does with regard to the wars undertaken by Louis XIV, that the poor bear the greatest burden; they receive the full impact of the privations which can be avoided or circumscribed by the wealthy.

> Les pauvres sont toûjours à plaindre; la perte n'est jamais que pour eux: dans quelque état qu'on soit, quand on est riche, on se tire d'affaire.

As Challe realizes more fully the implications of these reflections, he formulates a startling question: "Sont-ils [the sailors] moins hommes que les autres?" He readily admits that his experiences around the world have altered his perception of poverty:

> Je regarde à présent la pauvreté, avec bien plus de compassion que jamais; quoi que je puisse dire, que je l'ai toûjours regardée sans mépris. (J II, 117–18)

Life on the sea provides a setting for extensive human suffering through the natural elements, exposure to hostilities, perhaps open warfare. One of the principal forces of nature with which the sailors must struggle is the wind, which controls the ship's progress. Almost every page of the *Journal* refers to the importance, if not the dangers, of this natural force:

> Nous mouillames hier au soir, parce qu'il n'y avoit point de vent. La Lune étoit dans son plain. . . . Je ne sai si elle est cause du mauvais tems que nous avons eu. Nous étions, &

> sommes encore, à l'ancre. Il a fait toute la journée tourmente de vent. . . . Le vent & la marée sont trop forts: il nous a été impossible de lever notre ancre. Il fait beaucoup de vent d'Est-Nord-Est, une pluye très grande, & nos Matelots mouillés comme des barbets ne peuvent plus travailler; & le pis de tout, c'est que le tems est si sombre, que nous ne voyons pas à un quart de lieue de nous. . . . Il nous pousse sur les Côtes du Mogol, contigues au Pegu, dont nous sommes fort proches. En un mot, nous sommes très mal: Dieu veuille nous en tirer.

The powerful thrust of water currents, the inescapable rays of the tropical sun and its heat also affect the sailing and the lives of the sailors.

> Le vent est toûjours directement contraire, & nous ne voyons pas devant nous: ajoutez à cela, que peut-être les courans nous dérivent du côté que nous ne voulons pas aller, n'y ayant que faire; que la chaleur est si étouffante, que nous ne pouvons presque pas respirer (J II, 248–50)

Such references to the ill effects of the tropical heat occur with frequency throughout the *Journal*:

> Il fait encore une chaleur excessive. Il y a longtems, que nous tournons le dos au Soleil: cependant, on ne peut respirer; & si les pluyes ne tempéroient pas l'ardeur de ses rayons, chacun pouroit chanter 'Encore un tour de broche, & je suis cuit.' (J I, 359)

This excessive heat causes the death of more than one member of the crew:

> Il est mort cette nuit un de nos Matelots. La chaleur tue; & lorsque la fiévre s'en mêle, la maladie est courte. (J II, 117)

When the fleet arrives at the island of Chadube, west of Siam, on November 21, 1690, many of the crew are too ill or weak to work. "Notre Navire ressemble plûtôt à un Hôpital, qu'à un Vaisseau de Guerre" (J II, 319).

During the return voyage the fleet was engulfed by "un

coup de vent terrible." Work aboard ship was impossible; Challe was unable to write his daily log.

> Je n'écrivis point hier, ni avanthier, parce que je ne l'ai pas pu. Nous avons essuyé Jeudi, Vendredi, & hier Samedi, ce qu'on appelle à la Mer un Ouragan.

During this storm all members of the crew and ship's staff were in constant peril. "Nous avons cru cent fois, que le derriere de notre Navire alloit être emporté" (J III, 202–03).

A purely human peril, one no less real or threatening than those imposed upon man by the forces of nature, was the danger of attack at sea by pirate vessels or ships belonging to political enemies or commercial rivals. For Challe, only "la défense naturelle est légitime et de droit"(M 83). Wars of aggrandizement, battle for power and wealth involve human suffering of immeasurable proportions. Challe views such enterprises as instruments of human degradation and useless suffering. It should be recalled that Challe took part in the Battle of La Hougue (1692) between French and English maritime vessels. He witnessed outstanding examples of human suffering matched by Christian virtue. In the course of the battle, the French ship *L'Admirable* was abandoned. Her officer, Rillard, went aboard at least three times in order to save sailors and crew. "Il en sauva même plusieurs d'autres navires, qu'il ramassait à la mer." This act of heroism was so admired by the English that they held their fire.

> Les ennemis admirèrent cette charité et la respectèrent assez pour ne plus faire feu sur lui à son troisième retour.

In the end, the English burned fourteen French ships. The vice-admiral of the English fleet wrote to the leader of the French, M. de Tourville,[9] sending him his compliments

---

[9] "Anne-Hilarion de Cotentin, comte de Tourville, né au château de Tourville (Manche) en 1642, mort à Paris en 1701. Entré dans l'ordre de Malte en 1656, embarqué sur les galères, il se distingue dans les courses contre les

> sur sa défaite, qui lui était plus glorieuse que le succès au vainqueur, parce que celui-ci n'était dû qu'à la supériorité des forces, tandis qu'il ne devait sa longue résistance qu'à sa propre bravoure.

Immediately following the surrender, the two admirals met, unarmed, "sans autre précaution que leur parole réciproque." In this relationship, Challe notes heroism, respect for the individual and Christian charity.

> S'il est ainsi, j'appelle cela faire la guerre en honnêtes gens, qui indépendamment de l'intérêt de leurs souverains, rendent justice à leurs ennemis, les estiment et les aiment. (M 179–80)

These examples of valor and magnanimity do not obviate the harmful aspects of war. Challe clearly states his position vis-à-vis human suffering in time of war:

> Quel est le Souverain, qui voudroit entreprendre une Guerre, s'il étoit bien persuadé qu'il doit rendre compte à Dieu du sang qui y est répandu, & de tous les désordres qu'elle traine à sa suite? (J III, 356)

Misguided zeal which results in useless human suffering arouses Challe's indignation. If customs indigenous to a particular culture conflict with Challe's concept of the dignity and value of human life, he observes, analyzes, and describes the customs and offers his personal criticism. For example, during the layover of the fleet at Pondicherry, Challe becomes informed of the funeral customs of the natives. These idol-worshippers burn their dead; they also provide during forty days food and drink for the deceased. Challe's lengthy study of the funeral customs practiced by these people opens with the following scene:

Barbaresques. Capitaine de vaisseau, il seconde Beaufort dans l'expédition de Candie... Vice-Amiral des mers du Levant en 1689, il commande, sous d'Estrées, l'escadre chargée de soutenir Jacques II détrôné, débarque en Irlande et bat en 1690 près de l'île de Wight une flotte anglo-hollandaise" (M 172, note 1).

Quand tous ces Idolâtres meurent, on les brûle. J'ai vu à cinq ou six cens pas du Fort un corps brulé. Il y avoit deux pots de terre du côté de la tête, l'un plein de ris cuit, & l'autre d'eau.... Ces misérables s'imaginent que les morts y viennent manger & boire, pendant quarante jours; & c'est pour cela qu'ils y laissent cette provision, & que pendant cet espace de tems, ils y en apportent tous les jours de nouvelle. (J II, 179)

The plight of the widows of the Bramans deeply concerns Challe. Each widow must follow a prescribed code of behavior: she may not weep; immediately following the death of the husband, she must declare her intention to join him in the funeral pyre; she must persevere in this intention until her final moments. The funeral ceremony is ritualistic. The body of the Braman is carried in procession around the elevation of wood and then placed upon the bed-like structure. Other priests then file around the body, crying out and shouting lamentations; then, they take their places on the right and on the left of the body. Finally the widow appears, in the company of other women and young girls. She is dressed in festive garb:

La Femme parut ensuite, vetue de ses plus beaux ornemens, pleine de coliers & de brasselets, & enfin parée comme si elle avoit été à sa nôce. Elle avoit le visage riant, la démarche assurée, & rien ne témoignoit dans sa personne que la mort cruelle qu'elle alloit souffrir lui fit aucune horreur.... On lui fit faire trois fois le tour du foyer, sur lequel le cadavre étoit étendu: on lui demande autant de fois, si elle vouloit effectivement être brûlée avec lui? Elle répondit toûjours oui, avec beaucoup de résolution.

The widow mounts the funeral pyre, embraces the body of her husband, disposes of her garments and ornaments and takes her place at the head of the body. The account of these final moments is dramatic:

Jusques ici, il lui a été permis de se dedire; mais, elle ne le peut plus, si-tôt que le Braméne funeste éxécuteur d'une si terrible resolution, qui est monté avec elle sur le bucher, lui a

> lié le bras droit avec celui du mort. Ce Braméne se retire promptement, & promptement aussi les autres Braménes mettent le feu au bucher de tous côtez. On y jette du bois, & d'autres matieres combustibles: &, pendant ce tems, les Braménes, les Femmes, & les assistans font un bruit & des cris de tous les Diables; sans doute, pour empêcher de distinguer ceux de la patiente.

Challe strongly criticizes such customs which would result in an unjustifiable loss of human life. His summation of this funeral rite expresses his distaste for such usages.

> Ainsi, ce n'est que par un honneur ridicule, & une vaine ostentation, que ces Femmes se font mourir. . . . Leur mort est le fruit d'un zele mal conduit; mais cette mort est volontaire. . . . Il est cependant bien difficile que ces malheureuses Veuves s'en dispensent, étant poussées par une infinité de bigottes (il n'y a point de Religion qui n'ait les siennes) & par les fripons de Braménes, dont ces sacrifices volontaires de soi-même relevent la pretendue sainteté, & flattent l'amour propre. (J II, 183–88 passim) [10]

---

[10] There is a strikingly similar description of Eastern funeral rites in one of Montaigne's essays. The author refers to this custom in the context of his study of certain human strengths or virtues, "des traits miraculeux . . . qui semblent de bien loing surpasser nos forces naturelles." Montaigne describes the ritual followed by the most cherished wife of the deceased: "Un homme escrit encore de nos jours avoir veu en ces nations Orientales cette coustume en credit, que non seulement les femmes s'enterrent après leurs maris, mais aussi les esclaves des quelles il a eu jouissance. Ce qui se faict en cette maniere. Le mari estant trepassé, la veuve peut, si elle veut, mais peu le veulent, demander deux ou trois mois d'espace à disposer de ses affaires. Le jour venu, elle monte à cheval, parée comme à nopces, et d'une contenance gaye, comme allant, dict-elle, dormir avec son espoux, tenant en sa main gauche un mirouër, une flesche en l'autre. S'estant ainsi promenée en pompe, . . . en feste, elle est tantost rendue au lieu public destiné à tels spectacles. C'est une grande place au milieu de laquelle il y a une fosse pleine de bois, et, joignant icelle, un lieu relevé de quatre ou cinq marches, sur le quel elle est conduite et servie d'un magnifique repas. Après le quel elle se met à baller et chanter, et ordonne, quand bon luy semble, qu'on allume le feu. . . . [Elle] distribue ses joyaux et vestements à ses amis et se va plongeant dans l'eau, comme pour y laver ses pechez . . . . Finy qu'elle a de dire, une femme luy presente un vase plein d'huile à s'oindre la teste et tout le corps, lequel elle jette dans le feu, quand elle

Throughout the course of his travels, Challe is not only the representative of his nation and his Church and an open-minded and eager adventurer, he is haunted, like all travelers of his time, by the notion of the *Paradis Terrestre*. His travel accounts juxtapose social and political corruption, religious fanaticism and absolutism in government with sincerity, honesty and liberty. He is strongly attracted by the simplicity of the life of the Indians in Acadia. This theme is not new to French literature; Chinard describes in his study on *L'Amérique et le rêve exotique* the development of the idea:

> Le fait qui, à notre avis, apparaît comme le plus remarquable dans cette longue série d'ouvrages, est la continuité parfaite et le développement ininterrompu de la même idée dans toutes les relations de voyage. Le XVIe siècle avait reçu du moyen âge la vieille légende du Paradis Terrestre, et l'avait modifiée par des souvenirs de l'âge d'or empruntés aux poètes latins; dès la découverte même, la vision des voyageurs en avoit été déformée. Que certains aient retrouvé les gracieuses scènes des idylles antiques dans les Antilles et plus tard en Océanie, que d'autres se soient crus transportés au temps des patriarches ou aux premiers âges du christianisme, il y a au fond de toutes ces théories et de

---

en a faict, et, en l'instant, s'y lance elle mesme.... Le corps du mort est porté au lieu où on le veut enterrer, et là mis en son seant, la vefve à genoux devant luy l'embrassant estroitement." "De la Vertu," *Essais*, ed. A. Thibaudet, Livre II, chap. XXIX (Paris: Bibliothèque de la Pléiade, 1937), pp. 685 and 687–88.

Half a century after Challe's presentation of this ceremony, Voltaire describes the tradition through the fictional voyage of Zadig. In this description the focus is distinctive. Voltaire does not examine motivations for man's acts of heroism or virtue; his concern is not the waste of human life in the Eastern cultures. Voltaire exploits this Oriental ritual in order to call attention to contemporary social abuses in France. "Lorsqu'un homme marié était mort, et que sa femme bien-aimée voulait être sainte, elle se brûlait en public sur le corps de son mari. C'était une fête solennelle qui s'appelait *le bûcher du veuvage*. La tribu dans laquelle il y avait eu le plus de femmes brûlées était la plus considérée." This passage concludes with the satirical interrogation: "Y a-t-il rien de plus respectable qu'un ancien abus?" Voltaire, *Zadig*, XXI, 60.

tous ces tableaux, un élément antique, biblique et chrétien qu'il n'est pas possible de négliger. [11]

At first view the following description of the *point de départ* from which evolves the seventeenth century traveler's enthusiasm for the simple life of the natives in the New World may seem somewhat more poetic and visionary than the Challian accounts. However Chinard focuses on ideas which are central to Challian thought: individual liberty versus an absolute monarchy; fraternal charity versus barbarous warfare; natural virtue versus a superficially Christian ethic.

Souvenirs de l'âge d'or à jamais disparu d'entre nous et conservé miraculeusement parmi les sauvages de l'Amérique; rappels de Tacite, de Tite Live et de la république romaine, quand la liberté individuelle décroit et que la monarchie absolue grandit; beau rêve de fraternité universelle du christianisme primitif, au moment où les rois font la guerre sans consulter leurs sujets et contre les intérêts du pays; communisme monacal, observé par des paiens, morale exclusivement laïque, produisant des vertus supérieures à celles des civilisés; développement harmonieux du corps que nul vêtement ne vient cacher et que nulle tâche pénible ne dégrade et ne déforme; courses errantes et sans limites dans un pays béni où la nature est

---

[11] Gilbert Chinard, *L'Amérique et le rêve exotique dans la littérature française au XVIIe siècle* (Paris: Hachette, 1913), p. 431.
    Chinard further emphasizes the tradition of travel in European society. "On ne saurait trop répéter que le goût des voyages n'est pas un sentiment moderne, en France moins qu'ailleurs. . . . Il faudrait plusieurs volumes pour indiquer les titres des relations publiées au XVIIe siècle seulement, et beaucoup d'entre elles ont eu plusieurs éditions. Les annalistes de la conquête du Mexique et du Perou sont traduits et retraduits dans tout le cours du XVIIe siècle; les livres composés sur la Nouvelle France se montent à plusieurs centaines, et l'on en compterait presqu'autant sur les Antilles. . . . Notre expansion coloniale suffirait à prouver qu'au moins une certaine classe de Français continuait les traditions des grands navigateurs du XVIe siècle. Ceux qui ne voyageaient pas en fait, pouvaient au moins voyager en esprit, et . . . suivre dans les forêts du Nouveau Monde ceux qui l'on a appelés les pionniers français." pp. 189–90.

toujours douce, souriante et féconde, tels sont les principaux éléments du tableau mis sous les yeux des nations vieillies et fatiguées de l'ancien monde, par les annalistes du nouveau. [12]

Challe's work with the trading establishments in Acadia brought him into close contact with the life of the French colonists and a knowledge of the life of the Indians, namely the Iroquois. Twice within a single passage, describing the work common to both the colonists and the Indians, he advocates union of these two peoples. Such an alliance, incorporating the Indians into the life of the French colonies requires a strong base of mutual respect, loyalty and *bonne foi*. Challe specifically notes certain qualities of the Iroqouis which make of them suitable colonial colleagues: their friendliness, their innocence, and their adaptability. Challe describes

> les moeurs des sauvages, qui habitent ces lieux, leur innocence foncière, la facilité de vivre en bons termes avec eux et de s'en faire des amis, ainsi que la manière dont on pourrait les incorporer aux colonies, malgré leur éloignement pour notre religion.

He further notes the loyalty of this tribe, mentioning

> le loyauté ordinaire à ces peuples et qu'il fallait, pour se les attacher, les traiter avec une bonne foi réciproque. (M 263)

This commentary, theoretical in nature, is given a practical illustration and application by Challe himself, who, in the company of two Indian guides, crossed the snow capped mountains, Monts Sainte-Marie, separating Canada and Acadia.

> Je me souviens bien, que nous fûmes huit jours à monter, & cinq à descendre; & qu'il ne se peut rien de plus affreux dans le monde. Un Printems, ou plûtôt un Eté admirable, en bas: une brume ou un brouillard fort epais, ou de la pluie

---

[12] Chinard, pp. 219–220.

> fort menuë & bien froide ensuite; & un froid de tous les diables en haut, & si violent, que des poissons étoient pris & enchassez dans la glace, & de la neige de tous côtez, en sorte qu'à tous momens mes deux Sauvages & moi courions risque d'être abimez. (J I, 93)

This adventure clearly indicates that the Indians cooperate with those whom they trust:

> pourvu qu'on agisse avec eux de bonne foi et sans tromperie, car il n'y a rien que ces peuples abhorrent tant que la mauvaise foi. Ils se livreront sans reserve aux Français, s'ils les traitent avec douceur. (M 259)

Cooperation on the part of the Indians with the colonists, their possible "incorporation" into the colonies, does not imply a denial of their culture or customs. The case is totally contrary to such a view. Respect for individual differences and admiration for customs indigenous to a particular social group enable Challe to realize clearly that leaders must adapt to the customs of the people governed. In the context of the colonial foundations, Challe cites the example of M. de Saint-Castain, who merited the title of king of the savages, because he lived in accord with their customs.

> On pouvait, à juste titre, nommer [this Frenchman] le roi des sauvages, non seulement parce qu'il avait épousé une sauvage, mais par le crédit qu'il s'était acquis parmi eux, en vivant selon leurs coutumes. (M 263)

In the case of these simple people, living close to nature, Challe finds outstanding examples of goodness, humanity, and integrity.

> Qu'il s'agisse de moeurs sexuelles, de bonne foi, de bienfaisance ou même de religion, il [Challe] examine avec équité les usages des Indiens du Canada ou des Malbarais, et leur accorde ordinairement la préférence sur les Français. [13]

---

[13] Deloffre, "Robert Challe: Témoin de son temps," p. 97.

The innocence of the Indians in the New World does not prevent their recognition of self-seeking and dishonest dealings on the part of the French. Challe cites the signing of a peace treaty at which time the Iroquois refused entry to the Jesuits, considered by the Indians to be fortune seekers (M 93).

The humanity and charity of the Iroquois are illustrated in the account of their surprise attack and seizure of the city of Québec, governed by M. de Frontenac. At the hour of the attack, parents fled to a fortified chateau; children and the elderly were abandoned. The Iroquois

> ne touchèrent ni aux maisons ni aux meubles et ne firent aucun mal aux enfants, qu'ils nourrirent bien. . . . Ce qu'il y eut d'extraordinaire, c'est que lorsqu'ils retournèrent chez eux, ils emmenèrent ces enfants, et que lorsqu'ils les rendirent, par un traité de paix, ils étaient gros à lard, en meilleure santé qu'ils auraient éte dans leur famille, et qu'il n'en était mort aucun.

Challe's summary of the qualities of character manifested by the Iroquois is eloquent:

> Je ne vois, dans cette conduite, rien que d'humain et de généreux et rien de tout de cruel ni de barbare. (M 89)

Generally, Challe's estimate of the character of the peoples of the East is equally laudatory. He is especially emphatic with regard to the practice of the virtue of charity:

> tous les Peuples de l'Orient sont très charitables; & sur cet article, font honte aux Chrétiens. (J II, 211)

Challe describes the *Chandri*, or hospitals, with their medical resources and the kind service they rendered to the needy.

> Ils [the people of the East] entretiennent sur les chemins des Hopitaux, qu'ils appellent Chandri, où les passans, pellerins originaires ou etrangers, trouvent indifferemment ce qui leur est necessaire, suivant l'esprit des Fondateurs: c'est-à-dire, qu'il y en a, qui donnent du ris, d'autres du bois, d'autres de l'eau, d'autres des poules, d'autres des oeufs, & d'autres le couvert, & les pots & plats nécessaires; & que,

> dans tous ces Chandri, qui, à proprement parler, n'en font qu'un, n'étant qu'un même batiment, la provision est bientôt faite, tant pour les Hommes, que pour les bêtes, qui y trouvent aussi leur subsistance, & le couvert. (J II, 211–12)

The urban, commercial society of the Pondicherry strongly resembles Parisian society. Challe notes that members of the upper class solicit preferred posts for their children.

> Qu'un homme de qualité en Europe ait plusieurs enfans, l'ainé soutient la dignité de la famille: le second est destiné à l'épée, c'est un Chevalier de Malthe & le troisième est Monsieur l'Abbé.

In parallel fashion:

> Qu'un Banian ici ait plusieurs enfans, l'ainé soutient le Negoce & le Trafic du Pere: le second se met parmi les Neyres ou Gens de Guerre; & un autre se rend Bramène, ou prêtre des Idoles.

Challe views this social rigidity as indicative of the political and social ambition which he believes can infect every people: "Le Demon de l'ambition suit par tout sa même politique" (J II, 178–79).

Government officials in the East are also infected by this "demon de l'ambition." The officials in Bengal are Eastern versions of the ministers at the court of Versailles. Sent to Bengal from their native Agra, they consider the post "un honorable exil" because their seat of government is "éloigné de plus de trois cens lieues d'Agra, demeure ordinaire du Mogol." Challe reinforces this parallel with French government officials with the following generalization:

> tant il est vrai que, par toute Terre, les gens de distinction aiment à être proches de leurs Princes. (J II, 358)

Since Challe demonstrates deep respect for the traditions and customs of other peoples, he seeks to safeguard and preserve such cultural trappings. Cultural differences are positive social factors; they are not necessarily barriers; they do not, of themselves, separate. The somewhat humorous portrait of the native governor of the island of Saint Yago illustrates this serious attitude.

> Lorsque je le vis, il étoit vêtu à la Françoise. Je ne sçai s'il avoit sué de l'encre; mais son linge étoit bien noir. Il avoit des bas gris de perles, un escarpin couleur de noisettes d'un demi-pié plus long qu'il ne falloit, un justaucorps de drap gris de souris, une veste de satin de même couleur, tous deux brodez de fleurs de soye de toutes couleurs, très delicatement mises en oeuvres, à present fort fanées, & autrefois vives, & c'est ce qu'il avoit de plus beau. Une culotte de damas cramoisi serrée à l'Espagnole étoit dessous avec une épée au moins de six pieds de lame, avec une cane très belle, garnie d'argent, & sur tout d'une chaine très bien travaillée. Si bien, qu'en ajoûtant une reingrave à sa parure, il auroit fort bien representé l'original du Marquis de Mascarille des Précieuses de Moliere. (J I, 190–91)

Apart from the highly enjoyable spectacle afforded by this presentation, do not Challe's words also convey the serious conviction that observance of the normative customs and usages is not only fitting but preferable to a superficial adoption of new cultural patterns?

Months later, following his tour of Bengal, he restates this position vis-à-vis social customs. Having assumed the role of a Christian traveler, he enunciates several significant principles in the context of the Christian obligation to teach the message of Christ. First, he calls for simplicity in doctrinal presentation: "S. Paul ne prêchoit que Jesus-Christ, & ice-lui crucifié. Il a réussi. Pourquoi leur prêcher autre chose?" Second, he supports compromise with certain superstitions or beliefs indigenous to a given people:

> Il est impossible de défaire tout d'un coup les Payens, & les Idolâtres, de leurs Coûtumes; il faut de nécessité leur en souffrir quelqu'une de peu de conséquence, pour gagner l'essenciel. (J II, 365) [14]

---

[14] The remainder of this passage further illustrates this idea: "Les

Third, since the life of man is enriched by the use of symbols and rituals, it is advisable to develop customs which draw upon the character of native life and, at the same time, express Christian commitment. The example chosen by Challe to illustrate this last point is an especially beautiful one. The Bengali, converted to Catholicism, form the Sign of the Cross in such a manner as to retain qualities of Eastern culture:

> Leurs Signes de Croix, avec leurs deux mains pardessus leurs têtes jusques à leur piez, semblant une benediction qu'ils donnent aux autres, & un reste de leur ancienne salutation aux Idôles. (J II, 365–66)

The months at sea, the tours of different lands, experiences with varying cultures may have focused Challe's attention on the questions related to the origin of the human race. During the stopover at the Lesser Antilles, he formulates this question:

> D'où viennent ces Caraïbes? d'où viennent tous les autres Peuples qui habitent le Monde, & d'où viennent ceux qui habitent les Isles éloignées de tout Continent?

His musings lead to further questions, such as: "Sommes nous tous Descendans d'Adam & d'Eve?" and "Où leurs Enfans ont-ils pu s'étendre?" Challe wonders whether the descendants of Adam and Eve have migrated to distant lands prior to the Flood; he considers the problem of extensive inhabitation of the New World prior to the crossing made by Columbus.

> Nous n'avons aucune connoissance, que très moderne, du nouveau Monde. Il est cependant aussi grand que notre Continent, & par tout habité, aussi-bien que les Isles qui sont

---

Apôtres ont toleré quelques Ceremonies des Juifs pour les attirer plus facilement au Christianisme; & qui prétendroit défaire tout d'un coup les Peuples d'ici de leurs vaines Superstitions, ne gagneroit rien sur eux: c'est leur génie, ainsi que Plutarque l'a remarqué; 'Inclinant Naturâ ad Superstitionem Barbari.' Mais, c'est assez de tolerer une partie, la moins blâmable de ces Superstitions: on ne doit pas leur en inspirer d'autres."

séparées de lui, & de nous, par des espaces de Mer que nous
ne sçavons point que personne ait traversé avant Christophe
Colomb. D'où viennent ces Hommes & ces Femmes con-
formez comme nous? (J III, 358–60)

This idea of the unity and confraternity which exist
among men of all corners of the world is a basic theme which
runs throughout Challian travel documents. This commitment to the fraternal bond which unites all men is evidenced in
various contexts: the respect and tolerance manifested for the
customs and usages of all peoples; efforts to establish systems
of mutual cooperation for the greater benefit of all members;
the relationships and analogies cited which tend to minimize
cultural differences.

One of the strongest similarities noted and described by
Challe is the *rapport* between the customs of the idol worship-
pers of Pondicherry and the Christians of Rome. Challe states
that the religious practice of Pondicherry is "pleine de
. . . sotisses," but the natives have attributed to their idols certain virtues and heroic deeds. Challe is pleased by the analogy:

> Il est très vrai, qu'ils ne regardent point leurs Idôles comme
> un Dieu, premier Etre de tout, & que ce sont seulement des
> Hommes d'une Vertu eminente, qu'ils prétendent avoir été
> déifiés par leurs belles Actions; & positivement ce que dit
> Virgile, 'Quos ardens evexit ad Aethera virtus,' de même
> que les anciens Romains plaçoient dans le Ciel Romulus leur
> Fondateur, & ensuite leurs Empereurs. . . . Il me paroit que
> leurs Idôles sont parmi eux ce que les Saints sont parmi
> nous. En effet, ne sanctifions-nous pas ceux dont la vie nous
> paroit avoir été toute sainte? Le Pape ne les met-il pas dans le
> Ciel sur les Procès verbaux de leurs Vies? . . . Ne nous est-il
> pas ordonné de les reverer comme Saints? Ne les regardons-
> nous pas comme tels, & ne leur rendons nous pas un Culte
> tout Religieux, sur la Foi de Miracles quelques fois dou-
> teux, & souvent mal averez? (J II, 200–01)

This statement gains force and strength by the fact that it was
formulated by a devout member of the Christian community.
Challe's delight in cultural differences, his enthusiasm for

travel and discovery do not alter his conviction that all men, whatever their time period or geographical locale, experience the same basic needs and aspirations.

The years passed in travel have provided Challe with much data and a wealth of information. He has gained knowledge of lands and peoples; he has observed ceremonies and rituals; he has lived a new life. The theories and principles he develops on the basis of his travel experiences and impressions reflect his own social orientation: a respect for all men; a tolerance for the new and the different; an ability to adapt and compromise when necessary.

The final page of the *Journal* reflects Challe's joy and gratitude for a safe return to his native land. He is "heureux d'être de retour d'un si long Voyage, en bonne santé!" (J III, 410). In spite of Challe's enthusiasm for travel and the stimulation he enjoyed from new sights and experiences, he remains a loyal Frenchman, eager to regain his homeland. When *L'Ecueil* had set out for the Far East on the return voyage to France, Challe's *Journal* reads as follows: "Chaque pas que nous ferons desormais nous raprochera de notre Patrie" (J II, 316).

Chapter IV

Religion: A Tolerant Orthodoxy

While no single work of Robert Challe is centered on religious issues, each text reveals in some measure the religious questions of the time and his own attitudes, beliefs and commitments. Challe is a traditional believer who endorses religious orthodoxy and supports the concept of an institutional Church while proclaiming a liberal and democratic spirit in all matters, even religion. He cites three areas of major religious controversy and adopts openly and vigorously a position with reference to them. Because of his strong support of rights (individual as well as national), he is a proponent of Gallicanism.[1] He opposes any form of religious intolerance, particularly efforts to establish through coercion national religious unity. Lastly, Challe's approach to life is in direct contradiction to the tenets of Jansenist and Quietist teaching.

There is no hint in his writings of a desire to force his convictions upon others. Evidence points to a contrary conclu-

---

[1] Gallicanism is a principle held by a group of Catholics who, remaining faithful to Rome and to Church teaching, wished to achieve an administrative autonomy in the French Church.

sion: sincere respect for views which differ from his own. He does not exploit cultural differences in order to criticize contemporary French society. In establishing certain *rapports* between pagan religious ceremonies and Christian practice, he notes:

> Si je n'étois pas né Catholique, Apostolique, & Romain, si je n'étois pas connu pour aussi zélé pour ma Religion que je le suis par la Grace de Dieu, on pourroit dire que ceci sent le Libertinage." (J II, 202–03)

Since he asserts society's need for the Church, his proposals for the establishment of colonies in the New World presuppose a Catholic foundation. "La base . . . doit être la religion catholique, apostolique et romaine" (M 252).Challe adheres to the teachings of the Church; he enjoys membership and participation in the ceremonies and celebrations of this religious institution.

The three volumes of the *Journal* provide some of the richest material relative to Challe's religious convictions. Even the most casual reader of this lengthy work is impressed by the depth and scope of Challe's considerations of the meaning of life, the implications of eternity and the relationship between grace and the human will.

Many passages from the *Journal* illustrate Challe's adherence to the traditional practices and beliefs of the Church. There are references to liturgical practices and evidence of his participation in such ceremonies. Daily or frequent prayer forms an integral part of his life. The rhythm of life aboard ship includes the celebration of liturgical feasts. These are duly noted in Challe's account of the voyage to India:

> C'est aujourd'hui le jour de la Purification, ou de la Chandeleur. Notre Aumonier a prêché ce matin, & a pris son Texte du prémier Verset de l'Evangile d'aujourd'hui, qui est le 22 du second Chapitre de S. Luc. (J III, 186–87)

Challe participates in liturgical celebrations. As an instructed member of the Church, he is able to appreciate the richness of their symbolism. One such celebration is the Palm Sunday Procession:

> J'avois entendu la Messe à bord, je ne laissai pourtant pas d'assister à l'Office. C'étoit hier le Dimanche des Rameaux. Les Palmes, que tous ces gens portoient dans leurs mains à la Procession, me firent souvenir de l'entrée triomphante de Jesus-Christ dans Jerusalem. (J I, 194)

There is a tone of familiarity and ease in Challe's references to Church practices: daily Mass aboard ship, celebration or mention of feast days of the saints, sermons and shipboard prayers. The third volume of the *Journal* opens with New Year's greetings and prayers for the coming year (1691).

> Je viens d'assister à la Messe, & après avoir donné à Dieu les premiers momens de l'année, je donne les seconds à mes bienfaiteurs, à ma famille. (J III, 1)

Only as a member of the Church, secure in his beliefs, can Challe joke about certain practices. He recounts a humorous scene which took place aboard *L'Ecueil* en route to India. Prior to the close of Holy Week, the captain of *L'Ecueil* had carefully counted and locked the entire stock of table wines. "Tout cela se fait en riant." However, this strategy did not succeed: "Monsieur de la Chassée [one of Challe's companions], qui a vû tout ce badinage, a caché deux bouteilles plaines sous sa robe de chambre." All others aboard ship fasted except the ship's captain, M. Hurtain, M. de la Chassée and Challe:

> Tous les gens de la table, Capitaine, Officiers, Missionnaires, & autres Passagers, avons jeuné comme des Anacorètes, au pain & à l'eau.

This same easy attitude permits well-meaning criticism of the sermons of the ship's chaplain:

> Notre Aumonier nous a fait cet après midi un Sermon sur la Passion, & nous a tous menacez de nous en faire encore un autre le jour de Pâques, sur la Résurection du Sauveur. Tant

> pis, s'il tient parole, & qu'il soit aussi long que celui d'aujourd'hui [Good Friday]; car, quoi qu'il soit bon Religieux, bon Ecclesiastique, & sçavant, il n'est certainement pas bon Orateur, & je ne suis pas le seul qu'il ait ennuyé.

This account concludes on a note of raillery. Sailors and chaplain are the focus:

> Il n'a satisfait que les Bretons; ce qui n'est pas difficile. Qu'un Prédicateur parle beaucoup des Anges, des Saints, & du Diable; qu'il les mêle ensemble en fricassée, ou en salade . . . il a toûjours fort bien rempli son Action. (J I, 229–31)

Such passages quoted do not indicate that Challe mocks his religion or its practices. As a child of the household, he has the right to play and to work, to share the joys as well as the penance. More numerous in his writings than such bantering passages are those pages where he is serious and reverent. For example, during a stopover at Moaly, en route to the Far East, he witnesses the prayer services of the natives in one of their oratories. He believes the religion of the natives to be "composée du Mahometisme Arabe & de l'Adolatrie." His reaction, a serious one, is one of wonder and self-incrimination.

> Je fus mortifié de ce qu'une Adoration si fervente & si attentive ne s'addressoit pas au vrai Dieu . . . mais si cela m'inspira une vraie douleur, l'édification, que ces Peuples me donnerent par leur ferveur & leur receuillement, m'en causa une bien plus vive, & me fit sérieusement réfléchir sur la maniere dont vivent les Chrêtiens.

In this passage Challe clearly articulates the significance of the Real Presence, a basic teaching of the Church.

> Nous croyons, ou du moins nous faisons semblant de croire, que le Saint des Saints, le Créateur de toutes choses, en un mot, Dieu lui même, repose dans nos Tabernacles. (J II, 62–65)

In the fictional world of *Les Illustres Françoises*, one of the characters created by Challe speaks with the same reverence of the Real Presence. At the time of his dramatic marriage with

Clémence, heroine of the third tale, the young cavalryman, Terny, announces to the father of his bride: "Voilà votre fille que j'accepte pour ma femme en présence de Dieu même, qui repose dans le plus auguste de nos sacrements" (IF I, 166).

Such thoughtful presentations reveal a reflective man committed to the traditional teaching of the Church. Several other passages written during this sea voyage to India further illustrate the meditative side of Challe's character. At certain moments aboard *L'Ecueil* Challe finds himself a silent, solitary spectator of the sea world.

> Il me sufit de me mettre dans la grande Chambre du Vaisseau à une fenêtre, ou en haut de la dunette, ou à un des sabords de l'arriere dans la Sainte Barbe, & de regarder le gouvernail du Navire, pour me jetter dans une méditation profonde, & pour m'inspirer une espece de melancolie, qui jusques ici m'a été inconnue.

As Challe continues to look upon these waters, they take on a deeper meaning. The stirrings of the waters recall the movements of Divine Grace in the soul of man. He expresses his thoughts in a somewhat stereotyped manner.

> Je regardois les mouvemens de l'eau au tour du Governail, comme de simples effets naturels d'une eau repoussée ou retenue.... Présentement, je regarde ces mêmes agitations de l'eau comme une peinture & une image de la vie. Plus j'y fais de reflexion, plus j'y reconnois de raport.

These movements are caused and controlled ("une eau repoussée ou retenue") by the rudder, the ship's directional mechanism. Plotting a course through the waters places a ship in the path of certain currents and in opposition to others, thereby setting up ripples and movements in the waters. There is no hint in this consideration of the frightening aspect of the sea, its vastness, its emptiness, or its powerfulness. In the Challian view, the sea is the ocean of life ("une image de la vie"), always subject to the control of the helmsman. The ship's pilot directs the course and handles the movements and agitations of the waters stirred by the ship. The rocking and rolling of the waters support the vessel. Despite the threat of storms and of events unforeseen and unforeseeable, these waters offer a sense of security and well-being. There exists a natural relationship between the vast waters and the ship facing untold adventure. These waters are the natural habitat of the ship. A man at home on the sea, Challe finds this a most comfortable image. Challe draws an age-old analogy between this sea image and the earthly life of man. His development follows the lines of traditional Christian teaching. He sees this image as a reflection of the individual steering his course through life; he understands earthly life as the natural habitat of man, providing him with necessary support and comfort. Man is endowed with the requisite capacity to direct intelligently and wisely his course through life. As the ship is furnished with its rudder as a means of self-direction, man is endowed with intelligence and will which make possible his self-directed course through life.

This consideration is immediately followed by a passage dedicated to the subject of divine grace, an emanation of Divinity and symbolized by rays of the sun. As Challe ponders the mysteries which surround the life of man, he notes the spiritual quality of human nature. He also underlines the intimate participation of man in Divine Life.

> Notre Ame est un élixir de la Divinité, ou, si l'on veut, une emanation: Dieu l'a formée & créé de toute Eternité; & l'a mise en place, lorsqu'il l'a voulu. (J I, 135–37)

These images arising from the contemplation of the sea recur over a century later in the prose of Chateaubriand. The vast expanse of the waters of the sea, the limitless horizon inspire Chateaubriand's consideration of human and Divine life:

> Oh! qu'alors les aspects de l'Océan sont grands et tristes! Dans quelles rêveries ils vous plongent, soit que l'imagination s'enfonce sur les mers du Nord au milieu des frimas et des tempêtes, soit qu'elle aborde sur les mers du Midi à des îles de repos et de bonheur. . . . Dieu des chrétiens! . . . Des millions d'étoiles rayonnant dans le sombre azur du dôme céleste, la lune au milieu du firmament, une mer sans rivage,

l'infini dans le ciel et sur les flots! Jamais tu ne m'as plus troublé de ta grandeur que dans ces nuits où, suspendu entre les astres et l'Océan, j'avois l'immensité sur ma tête et l'immensité sous mes pieds! [2]

This life, this "élixir," to which Challe refers in orthodox terminology is grace. Divine grace is as generous and pervasive as this body of light. Challe writes:

> Je regarde la Grace comme le Soleil, qui éclaire également tout le Monde. Le jour est composée de vingt-quatre heures: ... la Zone torride, où nous allons entrer, ne jouit que pendant douze heures de la vue de cet Astre, peu plus, peu moins, suivant son éloignement ou son approche d'un Tropique à l'autre. ... Les Peuples qui habitent sous les Poles sont privez de la presence du Soleil pendant six mois de l'année; mais, pendant les autres six mois, ils jouissent de son aspect sans interruption. Ainsi, de quelque côté qu'on prenne le Globe de la Terre, & les Peuples qui en habitent la superficie, chacun jouit également pendant une année un jour portant l'autre, de douze heures de Soleil visible, & de douze heures de nuit, qui font les vingt-quatre dont le jour est composé.

No man is deprived of the grace needed for his salvation. At times grace may be more abundant than at others; in the course of life, man receives all that he needs. His is the responsibility to listen, to respond to the promptings of this grace, to heed his conscience which instructs him regarding the good or evil of his proposed acts. Challe sees that in the working out of Providence some good can emerge from evil. His thought on this subject is summarized by a quotation from St. Augustine:

> Ne putatis esse in vanum malos in hoc mundo, nam malus ita vivit ut corripiatur, vel ut per ipsum boni exerceantur. (J I, 120–21)

---

[2] Chateaubriand, *Le Génie du Christianisme*, in *OEuvres complètes*, (Paris, F. Didot Frères, 1842), III, p. 58.

Aware of man's need of grace, Challe also acknowledges the limits of human knowledge. His admission is simply a statement of fact made by one capable of accommodating himself to his life situation:

> Telle est sur la Nature la foible connoissance de l'homme. Sa plus forte & sa plus profonde spéculation ou méditation le ramene, malgré lui, à ce que disoit Monsieur Grandin, Doyen de Sorbonne, & l'un des plus sçavans hommes du monde, "Unum scio, quod nihil scio." (J I, 139)

In the text of one of his letters to the editors of *Le Journal littéraire de La Haye* Challe further expounds his views on the mysteries and secrets of the Godhead to which finite man lacks access.

> Je tiens à ce sentiment tres-certain et tres-orthodoxe, mais je ne croi point que les hommes puissent entrer dans les secrets de la providence. Je tiens meme que c'est une impiété formèle de vouloir les approfondir. Pompée dit dans la Pharsale de Lucain traduite par Brébeuf . . . 'Qu'un juste respect l'empêche de chercher Un secret que le Ciel a voulu lui cacher.' " (C 157)

Although familiar with many of the theological writings of his day, Challe does not take part in the controversies arising from differing views about the nature of grace or the kinds and efficacy of grace.

> Puisque je suis en train, & que je n'ai rien à faire, qu'à m'entretenir moi-même, il faut que je dise mon Sentiment sur la Grace. Mon sentiment n'est nullement d'entrer dans les Disputes de Monsieur Arnauld avec Monsieur Claude, ni dans celles du même Monsieur Arnauld avec les Jésuites au sujet de la Grace, du Libre-Arbitre, ou de la Prédestination. (J I, 115)

He finds such verbal jousts unnecessary as well as unfruitful. His method of stating this view is original.

DIXAIN

Ces Jeux de Mots & de Paroles
Scandalisent tout vrai Chrêtien;
Disputes d'autant plus frivoles,
Qu'au salut elles ne font rien.
Pourquoi troubler la Conscience
D'un Chrétien, qu'une humble ignorance
De tout orgueil a préservé?
Et qu'a-t-il besoin de connoître
Par quelle Grace il est sauvé,
Quand Dieu lui fait celle de l'être?

Paraphrasing Thomas a Kempis, Challe summarizes this thought: "J'aime beaucoup mieux être sauvé par la Grace de Dieu que de Sçavoir definir cette Grace" (J I, 123–24).[3] For Challe the possession of grace outweighs the ability to analyse it.

"Sauvé" for Challe, as for any orthodox Christian, implies life eternal or the immortality of the human soul. Challe draws much of his thought on the subject of eternity from a discourse delivered at a meeting of the *Société des Gens de Lettres et d'Esprit*, the literary group which he had known in Amsterdam. Challe was impressed by this presentation given by "un Abbé de ma connoissance, avec qui j'avois fait mes Etudes & suivi les mêmes Classes au College de la Marche." The detail with which he records the speech attests to his attention and

---

[3] Thomas a Kempis writes in his *L'Imitation de Jésus-Christ*: "J'aime mieux sentir la componction que d'en savoir la définition." Livre I, chap. I, p. 10 (Montréal: Granger Frères, 1910).

Challe's view is derived from the Pauline and Salesian tradition. "Si quelqu'un s'imagine connaître quelque chose, il ne connaît pas encore comme il faut connaître; mais si quelqu'un aime Dieu, celui-là est connu de lui." "Première Epitre aux Corinthiens," 8:2–3. Similarly, St. François de Sales, in writing of the science of salvation, declares that the man who believes himself instructed and who does not know how to save his soul lacks the most essential knowledge. Salesian spirituality teaches that it is better to use wisely the grace of God than to discuss and analyse its effects. Jean Camus, *The Spirit of St. Francis De Sales* (New York: Benziger Bros., 1910), pp. 382–83.

approval; his own words "si beau, si juste" prove his concurrence. The record of this discourse as transcribed by Challe stresses the unity existing between the nature of God and eternity:

> en parlant de l'Eternité, parlons de Dieu lui-même; puisqu'en effet Dieu étant éternel, l'Eternité n'a pu commencer que par lui, & avec lui.

Another passage of the discourse notes man's inability to comprehend the nature of God:

> Cette Eternité, que toute notre spéculation ne peut pas comprendre, doit être réunie dans Dieu. C'est lui seul qui est éternel; mais il a crée & mis en oeuvre toutes choses dans les tems differens que sa Sagesse l'a voulu.

The abbé concluded his presentation with a summation of the beliefs he held dear. These truths are also highly prized by Challe. The wording in this passage so closely resembles Challian thought that the reader is tempted to attribute this conclusion to Challe. The abbé stated that his intention was

> [de] prouver trois Véritez: la premiere, l'Eternité de Dieu, Créateur de toutes choses: la seconde, l'Immortalité de l'Ame: & la derniere, qu'une bonne action, faite par un esprit de charité, n'est jamais perdue, & ce sont trois Véritez, dont je suis parfaitement convaincu.(J I, 141–75)

  Eternity is the goal of man's earthly life. Between time and eternity there remains the potential stumbling block of death. In spite of orthodox teaching regarding the immortality of the soul, the act of dying, the physical separation from the natural world is, in Challian vocabulary, "un mal nécessaire" (J III, 209). There are several passages where Challe mentions a natural, human fear of death, especially a death caused by storms or accident over which man has no control. For example, he describes a near shipwreck:

> Oui, sans doute, on conçoit bien mal ces horreurs de la mort, lors qu'on ne la voit que de loin: il faut avoir été aussi près

d'en être la victime, que nous l'avons été pendant plus de cinquante-quatre heures, pour les bien comprendre. (J III, 209)

In this instance, Challe's thinking is colored by the circumstances in which he finds himself. His attitude is a natural one. His fears and apprehensions are based on his knowledge of the powers of nature over which he has no control. He is also strongly influenced by his own love of life. This does not negate his belief in eternal life and in immortality.

Eternal life implies and involves the cooperative efforts of man acting in accord with the promptings of grace. Basing his argument on the biblical account of the repentant thief, who was promised by the dying Christ, "En vérité, je te le dis, dès aujourd'hui tu seras avec moi dans le Paradis,"[4] Challe is convinced that man's sincere repentance will earn salvation. He recognizes the fact that the second thief dies unrepentant and evidently unsaved. Sincere repentance presupposes a special grace, a "Prédestination à la Grace gratuitement accordée" (J I, 117). However, man has an essential part to play even in the acquisition of that grace:

> C'est à nous, à nous servir des prémiers avertissemens qu'elle donne intérieurement à nos coeurs & à notre conscience; mais, si nous les négligeons, songeons d'en prévoir les suites. (J I, 130)

Man has the responsibility of heeding his conscience. In this context Challe quotes Corneille's *Polyeucte*, a play which provides a definition of grace and its relation to man: "J'ignore si Monsieur Corneille, lors qu'il a fait ses Vers, songeoit lui-même à définir la Grace; mais je sçai que c'est la plus belle, & à mon sens la plus juste définition, que j'en aye jamais vue."

---

[4] "L'Evangile selon Saint Luc," 23:43 in *La Sainte Bible*, traduite en français sous la direction de l'Ecole Biblique de Jérusalem. (Paris, Editions du Cerf, 1961).

> Ce Dieu, qui tient votre Ame & vos jours dans sa main,
> Vous a-t-il répondu de le pouvoir demain?
> Il est toûjours tout juste & tout bon; mais sa Grace
> Ne descend pas toûjours avec même éficace.
> Ces momens précieux, que perdent nos langueurs,
> Amolissent ces traits qui pénetrent nos coeurs.
> Le bras qui la lançoit se lasse, & se courousse:
> La force en diminue, & leur pointe s'émousse;
> Et ces traits fortunez, qui nous portoient au bien,
> Tombent sur un rocher, & n'opérent plus rien. [5]

Challe also stresses the importance of man's cooperation in his own salvation. This is the responsible liberty to which he refers when he asserts that God "veut que nous concourrions avec lui à notre salut." In confirmation of the efficacy of human effort, he cites St. Augustine, the Latin Father he greatly admires: "Qui fecit te sine te, non potest salvare te sine te." He reminds his readers that omniscience is an essential attribute of God "à qui rien n'est caché, ni passé, ni présent, ni futur." Arguing that the "Prescience de Dieu" in no way limits man's freedom of action, he quotes a phrase from St. Peter: "Secundum praescientium Dei Patris."[6] This fullness of divine knowledge does not force man to act, nor does it limit his field of activity:

> Dieu, à qui rien n'est caché, sçait ce que nous ferons; mais il ne nous impose pas la nécessité de le faire, il n'empêche point un homme d'agir en honnête homme, & ne l'empêche point non plus d'agir en scélérat, il lui laisse son Libre-Arbitre, & le choix & le pouvoir de faire bien ou mal, mais il ne lui impose point la nécessité de faire bien ou mal. (J I, 119–29)

Fully cognizant of human frailty, Challe nevertheless places stress on responsible, intelligent human activity. He respects the well-regulated life. He admits the commission of

---

[5] Pierre Corneille, *Polyeucte* in *OEuvres complètes*, 3 vols. (Paris: Garnier Frères), Vol. II, acte I, sc. v.
[6] "Première Epitre de Saint Pierre," 1:2.

certain follies which others (his readers) should strive to avoid. He exhorts others to select a way of life "plus réglé que le mien." His words imply a conviction that each man should formulate a series of principles which will serve to give direction to the decisions and activities of his life. The forthrightness with which he acknowledges his errors and mistakes gives no hint of Jansenistic fatalism. He writes "ma faute" without equivocation. Man carves out his own life; even on earth he can earn happiness or merit misfortune (M, Préambule, 2).[7]

Challe evaluates man's actions and reactions in a social context, affecting not only the individual agent but society as well. This awareness of the social group is a significant aspect of Challian thought brought to the fore by Catherine Lafarge, whose study of *Les Illustres Françoises* emphasizes the essential interdependence of human beings and their reliance upon one another for the resolution of certain differences or misunderstandings.[8] Challe is not a man to undertake a lonely enterprise. He believes in the value of concerted effort for the betterment of society and the individual. He enjoys life; he is thankful to be alive. This affirmation of God does not lead to the Jansenistic tendency of negation of self. The sharing of Divine Life is ennobling. Participation in the life of God, through grace, adds an infinite dimension to human endeavor.

Challe does not suffer the malaise which pervades the Jansenistic viewpoint. Nor does he illustrate Pascal's view of man's life:

> nous devons nous considérer comme des criminels dans une prison toute remplie des images de leur libérateur et des instructions nécessaires pour sortir de la servitude; mais il faut avouer qu'on ne peut apercevoir ces saints caractères sans une lumière surnaturelle; car comme toutes choses parlent de Dieu à ceux qui le connaissent, et qu'elles le

---

[7] This concept of man's responsibility is similar in tone to a maxim of Fénelon: "Il faut tout de même avoir des principes constants auxquels tous nos jugements se réduisent. Il faut savoir précisément quel est le but de la vie humaine." Fénelon, *Télémaque*, XX, 446.

[8] Lafarge, p. 121.

découvrent à tous ceux qui l'aiment, ces mêmes choses le cachent à tous ceux qui ne le connaissent pas. [9]

Nowhere in his life or writings are to be found the shadow of despair, the moral rigidity of the all-or-nothing teaching of the Jansenists. He is not tormented by the malaise of those who feel abandoned or unaided in their search of an unknown destiny. Therefore, it is difficult to account for the phrase which Augustin-Thierry applies to Challe: "frotté de jansénisme."[10] A similar view is held by Henri Roddier: "Mais il croit surtout en la fatalité, une fatalité qui n'est autre que la prédestination janséniste ... et calviniste."[11] Deloffre summarizes Challe's references to questions involving the delicate balance of free will and divine grace.

En bref, il se déclare pour le libre-arbitre et contre la prédestination, et ceci pour des raisons morales.... Ce qu'il admet, c'est la prescience de Dieu, mais sans attribuer à cette prescience 'aucune vertu ni force qui nous oblige d'agir, ni qui nous en empêche.' ... Il ressort clairement de tout cela, que, si notre écrivain est assurément de tendances 'gallicanes', on ne peut sans abus le dire 'frotté de Jansénisme.' (IF, Appendice, II, 584–85, note 31)

It is manifest that Challe places great importance on the responsibility of the individual to work out his own principles and to respond to graces offered him. As a member of the Church, man does not assume a passive role. His membership implies cooperation and work with leaders who, in turn, dedicate themselves to the service of mankind. The institution of the Church itself is designed for the service of man. This concept of service rendered man by social institutions is a keynote of Challe's view of government as well as the Church.

---

[9] Blaise Pascal, "Lettre à Mme Périer," *OEuvres complètes* (Paris, Seuil, 1963), p. 273.
[10] Augustin-Thierry, "Introduction," *Mémoires*, VIII.
[11] Henri Roddier, "Robert Challes, inspirateur de Richardson et de l'abbé Prévost," *Revue de Littérature Comparée*, 21 (1947), 31.

The parallel between these social organs is further developed through Challe's insistence that leaders dedicate themselves to the people. In Challe's study of government there are countless examples of criticism of the king, whose love of glory and personal ambition directed and dictated his decisions. There are also passages which criticize clergymen who, for reasons of personal ambition, seemingly do not fulfill their ministry. Such criticism, strong and frequent, is made of both the religious and secular clergy.

The question may properly be asked: Is such criticism in the spirit of orthodoxy? In Challe's case, the response is an unqualified "yes." The criticisms of absolutism exposed in an earlier chapter of this study are presented in behalf of the principle of monarchy. Similarly, a loyal member of the Church may well believe himself empowered, if not obligated, to note any deviation from the ideals of the institution.

Challe strongly condemns the avarice of members of clergy. He cites, for instance, the curé of Saint-Eustache as "l'homme du monde, qui sait le mieux secouer la bourse d'autrui et fermer la sienne." This same ecclesiastic, Challe recounts, refuses two bishoprics because their revenues do not equal the income from his rectory. Furthermore,

> son avarice augmente de jour en jour. Ses paroissiens sont les premiers à la plaisanter, surtout à propos des enterrements de maltôties. On dit que, pour l'argent il enterrerait un chien sous le maître-autel." (M 232–33)

Greed coupled with the profanation of sacred places is illustrated and condemned. The interment within the church proper of deceased members of wealthy families evokes a righteous anger on the part of Challe. His reaction is further proof of his abiding respect for the Eucharistic Presence on the altar:

> En effet, c'est une impiété, et même un sacrilège, de mettre la pourriture et le rebut de la nature, dans le même lieu où repose et où nous adorons le Saint des Saints. ... Les anciens conciles de la primitive Eglise, et même jusqu'au treizième siècle, défendaient absolument cette profanation.

> Ce n'est que l'avarice des gens d'Eglise qui a corrompu un si saint usage. (M 253)

Challe quotes additional cases in which priests, avid for offerings, carried out religious services without determining the will or intention of the recipient. For example, the case of a gentleman, Le Gendre, who died "sans foi, sans conscience et même sans religion" reveals that the curé of Saint-Eustache arranged and presided over elaborate funeral services. The curé "ne jugea pas bon de perdre les droits qui lui devaient revenir pour l'enterrement d'un traitant" (M 231–32).

In words which recall criticism of the lavish life of the king and nobles at the royal court, Challe attacks the powerful members of the clergy who live at the expense of the small parish or country priest. The distribution of funds and the allocation of lands were carried out with inequity:

> Comme ce sont eux [noble clergymen] qui en font la répartition dans leurs diocèses, ils font toujours si bien leurs comptes, que c'est le bas clergé seul qui porte toutes les charges; mais le train, ni la table de ces beaux seigneurs mitrés n'en sont pas moins somptueux, ni moins magnifiques.

Challes also believes that these clergymen compromised their religious ideals for their political security or advancement. They hesitated to speak out against abuses. Fearful of losing their comfortable position at court, they resorted to a "molle et lêche complaisance" (M, 14–16).

The final group of clerics examined by Challe is composed of members of cloistered and mendicant orders. Both types of congregations exist through public charity. They are exempt from taxation, even on their vast monastic land holdings. Challe evaluates negatively any congregation not actively engaged in society. Monks are the target of some of his most caustic comments:

> Les moines, de quelque ordre qu'ils soient, sont... des cruches, qui ne se baissent que pour se remplir et qui, peu à peu, s'emparent de tout le bien d'un Etat, sans en porter les charges.

Mendicant orders fare little better in the Challian evaluation:

> A l'égard des Ordres mendicants, ils les faut encore moins recevoir que les autres. C'est une taille réelle qu'ils perçoivent sur le peuple, d'autant plus cruelle et pernicieuse, qu'elle se lève sous le masque de la dévotion." (M, 244)

However, Challe clearly enunciates his position in favor of certain "active" religious orders. He recognizes the need in society for the contribution of dedicated clergy, positively engaged in the life of the people. The theme of confidence in and reliance upon the guidance of the family confessor or the parish priest is evident in at least two of the tales in *Les Illustres Françoises*. Challe's presentation of these clergymen is ordinarily respectful. He cites, for example, the case of Manon Dupuis, heroine of the first tale, who consults the confessor of her elderly father in her efforts to receive parental permission to marry. The prelate supports her request and tells M. Dupuis "tout ce qu'une rétorique charitable & chrétienne pouvoit lui mettre à la bouche" (IF I, 20).

A second instance occurs in the Contamine-Angélique tale. The heroine quotes the advice of her confessor: "Mon confesseur & mon sang m'ont toujours dit que la pauvreté n'étoit point un vice, & que devant Dieu & devant les hommes, une fille pauvre et sage est plus estimable & mieux reçûë qu'une riche libertine" (IF I, 80). Challe also endorses certain congregations whose *Rule* and way of life are geared to the alleviation of human suffering. Basic to this position is the belief, one to be developed fully in the eighteenth century, that work done for the public good is the source of well-being and happiness. Challe's plans for good government, presented in a quasi-utopian form of New World colonies, include the contribution of dedicated and self-sacrificing leaders; his recommendations for the spiritual domain is the admission to the colonies of religious groups, such as the *Frères de la Charité* and the *Religieuses hospitalières*.

> Je ne mets pas au nombre des moines et des moinesses, les *Frères de la Charité*, ni les *Religieuses hospitalières*. Ces derniers sont nécessaires dans l'établissement d'une colonie et pour

> ses progrès. Le soin qu'ils prennent des malades, à la fois pour l'âme et pour le corps, est un travail rude, qui les rend fort utiles. (M 245)

The reader becomes acutely aware that Challe fundamentally supports the ministers of the gospel. Any criticism leveled at specific groups or individuals flows from two sources: his innate respect for the ordained priesthood and many contradictions between the professed ideals and activities of the clergy.

It must be said that Challe reacts too violently against the Jesuits as a religious order. While their power at court cannot be underestimated, their role as dedicated missionaries should not be denied. Challe, however, loses no opportunity to excoriate individual members of the Society of Jesus as well as the spirit of the entire Society. Two Jesuit advisors and confessors at the court of Louis XIV are characterized in the following manner:

> Le Père de La Chaise et le Père Le Tellier, qui lui a succédé, étaient tous deux des fourbes trop parfaits pour agir avec droiture. (M 14)

During trips to Canada, Challe had occasion to observe the work of the Jesuits in this part of the world. He presents Jesuit missionary activity as motivated by avarice and self-seeking.

> Pour moi, qui ai suivi ces Peres, & examiné leur conduite dans le Canada, je suis absolument persuadé, que ce n'est que le Commerce, & le plaisir des sens, qui les mene si loin; & nullement le zêle de la Propagation de la Foi, ni l'envie d'attirer les ouailles dans le bercail du bon Pasteur. Je veux pieusement croire, qu'il y en va quelques-uns par ce seul motif; mais, l'experience m'a prouvé que cette vue de quelques particuliers ne forme pas l'esprit de la Societé en général. Et cela me paroît d'autant plus vrai, que la même expérience me montre, que ceux de leurs Peres, qui meurent dans ces Païs Sauvages d'une morte violente, mais pourtant bien meritée, & dont ils sont toûjours des Saints en Europe, ne sont véritablement Martirs que de leur lubricité & de leur avarice. (J I, 390–91)

Since Challe's assessment of the Jesuit missionary activities is seemingly severe and contrary to documentation compiled by historians,[12] it is difficult to ascertain the facts of the case. Certain critics note a strong prejudice in Challe's remarks concerning the Jesuits.[13] However, it is difficult to accept the validity and accuracy of Challian political and social criticism and his study of the role of the Church in his society and, at the

---

[12] "Without the Jesuits, French Canada would have been nothing more than a few trading-posts. It was their aim to follow the traditions of Spain in converting the races of the lands they occupied. But they actually went further than this, by outstripping the other settlers, and going to live alone among the natives. Their task was formidable. . . . The rigidity of their religious discipline was an asset in the missionary field, where men of action, with courage based on faith, carried the Cross into hostile lands, and, by bringing them medical comforts, showing them where to settle and how to farm, attracted the Indians to the Christianity which they advertised in so practical a manner." Geoffrey Treasure, *Seventeenth Century France* (Doubleday and Co., Garden City, 1966), pp. 116–17.

A Protestant historian from New England describes the seventeenth century Jesuit missionaries to Canada as follows: "These were no stern exiles, seeking on barbarous shores an asylum for a persecuted faith. . . . A fervor more intense, a self-abnegation more complete, a self-devotion more constant and enduring, will scarcely find its record on the page of human history." Jesuit relations with the Indians were founded on respect: "While laboring at the work of conversion with an energy never surpassed, and battling against the powers of darkness with the mettle of paladins, the Jesuits never had the folly to assume towards the Indians a dictatorial or overbearing tone. Gentleness, kindness, and patience were the rule of their intercourse. They studied the nature of the savage, and conformed themselves to it with an admirable tact. Far from treating the Indian as an alien and barbarian, they would fain have adopted him as a countryman." Francis Parkman, *The Jesuits in North America* (Boston: Little, Brown, 1886), pp. 83 and 134.

[13] Marchand writes of Challe's "excessif acharnement contre les Jésuites," and he further mentions that he "étoit si transporté de passion, ou, pour mieux dire, de fureur & de rage, contre cette Société, qu'on l'a plus d'une fois entendu s'écrier avec véhémence, que, s'il tenoit le dernier Jésuite, il ne feroit aucune difficulté, pour en délivrer une bonne fois le monde." p. 186.

In the "Introduction" to his edition of the *Mémoires*, Augustin-Thierry declares that "C'est principalement aux Pères de la Compagnie de Jésus 'ces reverends messieurs,' comme il les nomme, que s'adressent toutes ses fureurs." VIII.

Deloffre writes of his "haine des jésuites" as one of the principal themes of Challe's *Mémoires* (IF, Introd., I, XXXIII); he further qualifies him as "un adversaire résolu des jésuites" in his article, "Robert Challe: Témoin de son temps," p. 91.

same time, reject his judgment of the Society of Jesus. A basic question is: What is the origin of Challe's excessive hatred of the Jesuits? The cause may be a purely personal one; it may be a matter of political principle, for Challe's Gallican stance would place him in direct opposition to the ultramontane party. His reaction to ultramontanism is openly hostile: "Il n'y a qu'une poignée de canaille, qu'on appelle les Docteurs Ultramontains" (J III, 35).

Challe asserts that the Jesuits at the court of Louis XIV were partially responsible for the decision to revoke the Edict of Nantes. This single act was the culminating point in efforts to establish unity of religion throughout the nation. Decades of dissension, discord, and suffering, stemming from injustice and intolerance, preceded the signing of the Revocation. The outcome, discussed in detail in an earlier chapter of this study, was negative: serious social and economical problems developed; no significant progress toward religious unity was discernible.

Examples of religious intolerance, fanaticism or coercion are deeply disturbing to Challe. While in Portugal he witnesses the Atto dà Fè:

> J'ai vû a Lisbonne leur Atto dà Fè, ou leur Acte de Foi. . . . Les Portugais sont les Diables, qui perfectionnent la vive Peinture de l'Enfer des Payens.

He is also properly angered by the "indigne & éxécrable Tribunal de l'Inquisition, qui entretient, multiplie, & fomente" a series of abuses and whose misuse of power "étouffe la Parole du Sauveur." Any form of profiteering from religion, any suggestion of superstition, is also unacceptable to Challe:

> Tous ceux qui, comme moi, ont été en Portugal, sçavent que ce n'est plus la Religion de Jesus-Christ, qui y prime; mais, seulement, celle des Moines, qui la font consister en Indulgences, en Reliques, en Images, en Confrairies, en cordons, en Chapelets, & autres Babioles condamnables par leur excès. (J II, 364–65)

While Challe presents the subject of papal infallibility as

if this were a superstition promulgated by the Church and therefore finds no reason to support such a concept, it should be noted (if only in behalf of Challe's orthodoxy) that the official teaching on this subject was not proclaimed until 1870 at the Vatican Council.

> Jamais Pape mortel n'a été & ne sera jamais infaillible. Je regarde comme des Impies ceux qui ont le front d'attribuer à un Mortel, qui a besoin d'un Confesseur, l'Infaillibilité, qui après la Bonté, est le plus bel attribut de Dieu qui seul est infaillible. (J I, 110)

In order to reinforce this view, Challe makes a second reference in the following volume of the *Journal* in which he refuses to attribute to any pope "cette Infaillibilité, qui ne se trouve qu'en Dieu, & nullement dans un Homme mortel, pecheur comme un autre" (J II, 156).

Challe explores another area in which ecclesiastical authority can be abusively operative: the cloister. It was not uncommon practice for parents to force their children (or the youngest child) to live the monastic or cloistered life. In Challian thought, such infringement on the liberty of an individual is reprehensible; the compliance of the religious community in question is equally blameworthy. Challe's presentation of this matter prepares the way for the work of Diderot, over half a century later, in the novel, *La Religieuse*. Although she enjoys a happier fate, Clémence Bernay, the young heroine of the third tale in *Les Illustres Françoises*, may be considered one of the precursors of Suzanne. Her life is marred by two factors: her unwillingness to accept that life, and the pressure exercised by her parents.

> [M. Bernay] avoit promis à la Communauté de la faire bienfaitrice, si on pouvoit l'obliger à se faire religieuse. Il avoit offert pour elle une dot si forte, que ces bonnes dames pour ne pas laisser échaper un si grand fonds l'avoient persécutée & enfin obligée de prendre l'habit. (IF I,157)

Late in the seventeenth century, La Bruyère also writes vehemently against forced religious vocations:

> Une mère, je ne dis pas qui cède et qui se rend à la vocation de sa fille, mais qui la fait religieuse, se charge d'une âme avec la sienne, en répond à Dieu même, en est la caution. Afin qu'une telle mère ne se perde pas, il faut que sa fille se sauve. [14]

There is, however, a counterpoint to this criticism of the political and financial manoeuvres of certain religious congregations. Such abuses are not necessarily the fault of religious life, but the responsibility of the members of these orders. In the working together of the seven tales of *Les Illustres Françoises*, the figure of Gallouïn (the seducer of Silvie in the sixth tale) becomes important. Ashamed and repentant (upon learning of Silvie's secret marriage), he withdraws to a monastery. Through this character, Challe may well have expressed his definitive position on the question of religious vocations. The speaker in the following passage is the young Dupuis, the alter-Challe:

> Il [Gallouïn] prit l'habit à son retour, & fit ses voeux, après lesquels il me dit ce que je viens de vous dire de son voyage. Il a vécu comme un Saint pendant le reste de sa vie.... Je ne puis m'empêcher de faire une réflexion sur sa vocation & sa conversion: qui est, que si on ne recevoit dans les couvens que des gens véritablement repentans & convertis, le nombre des Religieux ne seroit pas si grand; mais leur vie seroit plus exemplaire & plus édifiante. (IF II, 520)

Any infringement or limitation on man's freedom of conscience is alien to the Christian ethic. Challe's respect for every individual and for the rights of the individual flows from his spirit of tolerance, his faith in human nature and his belief that man is capable of progress.[15] This commitment to man

---

[14] La Bruyère, II, 178–79.
[15] Pierre Bayle's appreciation of tolerance is Challian in tone; in his view "la tolérance est la chose du monde la plus propre à ramener le siècle d'or." Albert Cazes, *Pierre Bayle* (Paris: Dujarric and Co., 1905), p. 203. However, it should be noted that Challe's approach differs from Bayle's which is based on the spirit of free inquiry and on man's inability to arrive at certitude in matters of morality or religion. The contrary is true of Challe.

and his abilities becomes a central theme in the thinking of the eighteenth century *philosophes*. In the second half of the eighteenth century Voltaire summarizes the Christian view which underlies Challe's position: "De toutes les religions, la chrétienne est sans doute celle qui doit inspirer le plus de tolérance."[16] This announcement of an essential Voltairian theme, tolerance, is further illustration that Challe's religious ideas reflect the spirit of the evolving epoch of the Enlightenment.

Challe's *point de départ* is always the common man. An average citizen, a little known member of the bourgeoisie, he chooses to present his own ideas and his personal views. The focus of his attention is directed toward "the moral questions which arise from . . . commonplace situations."[17] The defense of the ordinary man is also explored by Montaigne, who chooses his own life and ideas as the subject of his writings: "Ce dessein de se servir de soy pour subject à escrire seroit excusable à des hommes rares et fameux qui, par leur reputation, auroyent donné quelque desir de leur cognoissance." Their subject matter is "digne et riche." Montaigne declares that his *Essais* are composed "pour le coin d'une librairie, et pour en amuser un voisin, un parent, un amy, qui aura plaisir à me racointer et repratiquer en cett' image." He finds the subject of his writings "si sterile et si maigre qu'il n'y peut eschoir soupçon d'ostentation."[18]

Challe's adherence to the teachings of the Church is tempered by his respect for each individual and his right or obligation to follow his conscience; his belief that the Church is a necessary institution in his society results in his study of ways and means to place the Church *at the service of the people*.

---

[16] Voltaire, *Dictionnaire philosophique*, XX, 521. A second passage in this article "Tolérance" is close in spirit to Challian thought: "Il est claire que tout particulier qui persécute un homme, son frère, parce qu'il n'est pas de son opinion, est un monstre." *Ibid.*, p. 520.

Diderot captures this view in a brief but strong definition of intolerance: "L'*intolérant* doit être regardé dans tous les lieux du monde comme un homme qui sacrifie l'esprit et les préceptes de sa religion à son orgueil; c'est le téméraire qui croit que l'arche doit être soutenue par ses mains; C'est presque toujours un homme sans religion, et à qui il est plus facile d'avoir du zèle que des moeurs." "L'Intolérant," XV, 240.

[17] Showalter, *Evolution of the French Novel*, p. 217.
[18] Montaigne, "Du Dementir," *Essais*, Livre II, chap. XVIII, p. 650.

Chapter V

Man: A Democratic View

The Challian concept of man's role in society is straightforward and simple: each individual (civil or ecclesiastical leader or ordinary citizen) has a responsibility to himself and to members of his society. This view of man's social responsibilities is presented in a democratic context; Challe views these social responsibilities from the perspective of a member of the bourgeoisie, actively engaged in commercial, colonial and maritime affairs. Each member of society is evaluated on the basis of his personal merit and qualities of character; his importance is proportionate to his industry, dedication and contribution to the general good. In such a social climate it is possible for man to improve himself, to rise in society and to assume posts of leadership. Man is not measured by social conventions such as fortune, family or position. Such usages are no longer operative; certain rigid conventions give place to more human values.

Challe is uncompromisingly committed to belief in man's freedom of choice. Man is responsible for his actions; he is accountable for his acts. It is, therefore, incumbent upon man so to direct himself as to develop his talents and abilities for his own welfare and for the good of society. Important as is the individual citizen, he is never viewed by Challe as an isolated entity; studied and presented as a distinct individual, he is also integrated into his society.

There are certain qualities which Challe considers eminently necessary for the full development of man's potential and his contribution to society. Honesty, far-reaching in its implications, is an essential social virtue. As understood by Challe, this single attribute encompasses such qualities as truthfulness, fair-dealing, sincerity and integrity. Its practice lays the foundation for meaningful and enriching relationships.

Personal references to honesty are numerous in Challe's writings. His *Journal* opens with a dedication to truth:

> Ce que je vous envoie est la Compilation de trois Journaux que j'avois faits, l'un pour Monsieur de Seignelai, le second pour Monsieur..., & l'autre pour moi. Il les comprend tous, & ne contient rien que de très vrai. (J I, 2)

Challe's respect for the property of others dictates his extreme care in safeguarding the possessions of the men who die aboard ship and his refusal to pillage. When the fleet arrived at Moaly, en route to the Far East, the natives of the island fled from their village, leaving the seacoast deserted. Strong was the temptation to steal some of the beautifully worked pieces of wood, carved and embellished by the natives.

> Il n'a tenu qu'a moi d'en prendre dans ce Village abandonné: peu d'autres auroient, comme moi, resisté à la tentation violente qui m'y poussoit; mais, en honnête-homme, je n'ai pas cru devoir mettre à profit la terreur panique du propriétaire: outre cela, le bien d'autrui n'est point à moi. (J II, 83–84) [1]

---

[1] These same words were addressed by Fénelon to the French king in reference to the wars undertaken during his rule, in particular the Dutch war, inspired by "un motif de gloire et de vengeance; . . . d'où il s'ensuit que toutes les frontières que vous avez étendues par cette guerre sont injustement acquises dans l'origine. . . . Il est inutile de dire qu'elles [conquests] étoient nécessaires à votre état: le bien d'autrui ne nous est jamais nécessaire." Fénelon, *Lettre à Louis XIV*, XXIII, 342.

The man who lives honestly and openly in a manner consistent with his beliefs is highly esteemed by Challe. M. Hurtain and two other officers aboard *L'Ecueil* merit his commendation. M. Hurtain is qualified as "un très honnête homme" (J I, 8). Furthermore, and more importantly, he exhibits a selfless courage in holding firm to his beliefs and commitments: he preferred imprisonment to the renunciation of his religion:

> [il] avoit mieux aimé soufrir les peines d'une longue & dure servitude, que d'accepter les offres qu'il [his patron] lui faisoit pour renoncer à sa Religion & se rendre Mahometan, & qu'il avoit méprisé les exemples qu'on lui présentoit, même de ses Compatriotes.

His was a soul "incapable de plier sous la force" (J I, 303–06).

The personal integrity and kindness of the other officers are noted by Challe:

> Il [M. Gouault] est sans contredit un des plus honnêtes hommes du monde, & des mieux faisans. Se probité égale celle de Monsieur Ceberet; je ne puis rien dire de plus fort pour en faire l'Apologie. (J I, 52)

Within the framework of the last tale of *Les Illustres Françoises*, Dupuis offers to the assembled listeners a mature definition of honesty. His eloquent words accentuate both the concept of personal integrity as well as the social implications of honesty. His remarks betray such deep convictions and firm commitments that they seem to convey the thinking of their author:

> L'honnêteté d'un homme, git dans sa sincérité, dans sa probité, dans sa bonne foi, dans une vraie compassion pour les malheureux, dans un retour sincére de tendresse pour les gens dont il est aimé, dans la reconnoissance des bontez qu'on a pour lui, & dans une stabilité fixe & inébranlable dans ses promesses. (IF II, 493)

Challe's examination of the social implications and significance of honesty and integrity is extended to an evaluation of the role of honesty in the problems of economy and in financial relationships among nations. In the private or public forum, the same principles underline his ethic. Dishonest dealings destroy the bonds which unite men and nations. He cites several examples of fraudulent financial transactions, particularly the practice of declaring bankruptcy in order to evade payment of debts. Challe blames both the businessmen involved in such practices and the indulgent judges and ministers of justice who encourage or permit this situation to persist.

> Ce n'est pas seulement le Commerce de la Hollande, qui a abatu le nôtre: c'est nous mêmes, qui y avons le plus contribué, & y contribuons encore la plus, par l'indulgence que les Juges ont pour les Banqueroutiers; auxquels, aux dépens d'un honneur que ces Scélérats ont foulé aux piés, la Justice en France conserve la vie. (J II, 369)

Trade with the East, established and maintained by the authority and integrity of the French monarchy, diminished when the credit of the *Compagnie des Indes* was permitted to declare bankruptcy.

> Les Orientaux se figuroient, que si elle [the *Compagnie des Indes*] ne les payoit point, ils n'auroient qu'à recourir à la Justice du Roi: mais ils ont bien changé de sentiment, parceque la Compagnie, ayant souffert des Banqueroutes, a été obligée de reculer les payemens; & les interêts courant toûjours, elle doit à present à Suratte environ six millions de livres, & y est tellement perdue de crédit, que qui que ce soit ne lui veut rien avancer.... Aussi, la nôtre [nation] y est regardée comme la plus fourbe & la plus indigne du Monde; & les lâchetez, qui se sont faites à Siam, nous vont faire regarder par toutes les Indes comme la plus vile canaille de la Terre.

This contagious spread of *mauvaise foi* is the direct cause of many commercial problems. The re-establishment of *bonne foi* between nations (and individuals) is an integral element in cooperative enterprise. Just as dishonest dealings disrupt and weaken relationships between individuals, they serve to break ties between nations.

> On verra que la mauvaise foi qui regne en France influe ici [Bengal]; & c'est où j'en voulois venir, pour faire finir à une Potente tous les Banqueroutiers, sans en excepter un seul, & du moins faire rouër vifs les frauduleux. (J II, 383–84)

Challe considers such insidious and devious practices more dangerous and destructive to the spirit of society than an overt act of thievery.

> Un voleur de grand chemin est moins à craindre dans le Public, & y fait sans comparaison moins de tort, qu'un Marchand de mauvaise foi. Le Voleur ne trompe pas la bonne foi, parce que personne ne s'y fie: le Marchand trompe la bonne foi & ses Amis les premiers. (J II, 369)

Since each member of society bears the responsibility to fulfill his role and to perform his tasks in view of the general welfare, a spirit of industry and a sense of accountability are essential qualities of the citizen actively engaged in the life of his society. Challe does not hesitate to tell his readers that his maritime officers recognized and praised his accuracy and industry:

> Tous deux me dirent, que si tous les Ecrivains du Roi tenoient un Journal, & un grand Livre, aussi exacte que les miens, & ne remettoient pas au bout du mois à prendre sur un seul feuillet les consommations des Officiers Mariniers, & qu'ils écrivissent jour par jour la qualité des rations fournies, le Roi épargneroit plus de deux millions, année commune, parce que les faux extraordinaires n'y pourroient pas entrer à la fin de l'Armement. Je puis me vanter qu'ils loüérent fort mon Journal, dans lequel ils virent jour par jour les Procès verbaux, les Inventaires, & les Consommations de guerre & de bouche. M. de Clouzeaux ajouta qu'il faudroit obliger tous les Ecrivains du Roi à tenir leur Régître comme j'avois tenu le mien. (J I, 44–45)

In further support of the esteem earned by his industry

and effort, Challe recounts an amusing anecdote. Several of the *écrivains du roi* from other ships in the fleet fell overboard. Challe is the only member rescued by the crew.

> En mon particulier, j'ai eu le malheur de tomber à la Mer, en sortant du Navire à Negrades: il n'y avoit aucun péril; mais je ne laissai pas de me voir secouru par plus de trente hommes, qui s'étoient jetté à l'eau. Cela me fit un plaisir d'autant plus grand, que deux autres dans le même poste que moi, ont été fort heureux de sçavoir nager, pour gagner terre. (J II, 328–29)

Challe often commends a specific individual who prides himself on the fulfillment of his duties and a task well done. Significantly, however, only one member of the regular clergy is so approved: the Dominican chaplain aboard *L'Ecueil*. Challe recognizes and comments upon the contribution of this priest to the short-term shipboard society: "C'est un bon religieux Dominiquain du Couvent de Morlaix.... C'est un bon homme" (J I, 101–02).

Industry, coupled with zeal and selflessness, characterizes the man whose contribution to society is noteworthy. Talents acquired through training and education, as well as experience are essential concomitants. Challe offers his readers a further description of the qualities of M. Ceberet, who earned the esteem of his colleagues and merited advancement in his career through

> son zêle inexprimable pour le service & les interêts du Roi, dans un travail infatigable, dans une application continuelle à ses devoirs. (J I, 51)

This officer was thoroughly trained in his career; he had long experience in maritime matters:

> Les fréquens voyages, que Monsieur Ceberet a fait sur Mer, lui ont acquis une parfaite & profonde connoissance de la Marine; ... en effet la Marine est un Art, qui, de quelque côté qu'on le puisse prendre, s'apprend toûjours beaucoup mieux par la pratique que par la théorie. (J I, 52–53)

In spite of a certain well founded hostility toward the colonial establishments undertaken in the New World by England, Challe is able to praise the selfless efforts of the English missionaries, whose zeal is disinterested and edifying:

> Malgré le tort que les Anglois m'ont fait, je leur rens avec plaisir la justice qui leur est due. Pendant que j'ai été leur prisonnier dans la Nouvelle Angleterre, j'ai trouvé des Sauvages fort bien instruits des véritez Catholiques. Ils ont des Ministres, qui ne s'occupent qu'à leur Instruction. Ce n'est certainement point en vûe d'aucun gain; car, ces Sauvages ne possedent, quoi que ce soit au monde. Ces Ministres s'y appliquent pourtant, & réüssissent infiniment mieux que ne font les Missionnaires, les Peres de l'Oratoire, les Jésuites, les Recolèts, & les autres, dans le Canada, qui est contingu. D'où vient cela? Oserois-je le dire? Oui. C'est que leur zèle est pur, ou que du moins il est dénué de l'esprit de Primatie & de Commandement, & sur tout d'Avarice & de Luxure. (J III, 40–41)

Courage in the face of great physical disaster or calamity, the willingness to risk one's life for the benefit of other men, are also qualities highly valued by Challe. M. de Porrières, who becomes the captain of *L'Ecueil*, is a man of such bravery. Replacing M. Hurtain, who died at sea on April 23, 1690, he is formally welcomed and warmly received aboard ship by officers and crew. His reputation for acts of heroism and his readiness to face personal danger earn the respect of his men:

> Il est très brave de sa personne, & s'est trouvé dans quantité d'Actions, tant contre les Turcs, que contre les Anglais & les Hollandois. (J I, 327)

Just as Challe studies the harmful social effects of dishonest dealings, he also cites instances in which self-interest or self-preservation, misguided or uncontrolled, can lead to fruitless human suffering. The outstanding and unforgettable example in the *Journal* occurs at the time of the battle with an English vessel, the *Philip-Harbert*, "l'un des plus beaux & des plus forts Navires qui fussent à la Mer." In order to prevent capture by the French fleet, the English captain sets fire to his ship. Then he rowed away from the flaming ship leaving crew, sailors and animals to perish in the inferno.

> Quelle horreur, de voir un Navire en feu! En un moment ce ne fut que flame! Quelle horreur, d'entendre les cris du reste de son Equipage, que ce malheureux avoit abandonné à une mort certaine! Quelle horreur, d'entendre le mugissement des animaux, consommez tout en vie! Ce Navire fut plus d'une heure & demie, qu'il sembloit un charbon ardent.
> ... C'est ainsi qu'à péri le Philipes Harbert, de Londres, ... par l'intrepidité & l'inhumanité de son Capitaine: digne assurément d'une meilleure fortune, s'il eut suivi le parti de son Prince; mais, homme à jamais condamnable, non seulement par cette raison, mais aussi par la cruauté qu'il a eue d'abandonner aux flames, & à une mort également certaine & horrible les mêmes hommes qui avoient si opiniâtrément secondé son courage & son désespoir.

Challe's summary remarks of this inhuman and unheroic act are unequivocal:

> Mais, j'ai une vraye compassion de ceux qui ont été brulez, ou du moins noyez, en voulant se sauver. Ceux, qui sont à terre, sont encore à plaindre. Qu'elle confiance peuvent-ils prendre dans un homme, assez barbare pour tout sacrifier à un honneur chimérique qu'il se fait à lui-même, & ceux même auxquels il doit cet honneur qu'ils lui ont acquis par leur bravoure. S'il s'étoit brûlé lui-même, son action auroit tenu de l'Héroïsme: mais, il s'est sauvé; & cela lui donne une autre face. (J II, 93–95)

The possibility of deep and lasting conversion is explored by Challe. Man is capable of improvement: experience, sudden disasters, or unforeseen events can serve to bring forth the best qualities of an individual. The case, par excellence, is "un nommé Mr. de Bouchetière qui se fait nommer le Chevalier." During the early months of the sailing to the Far East, Challe describes him in pejorative terms:

> Il n'y a que huit jours qu'il est revenu au Port-Loüis, & qu'il a trouvé le secret de se faire universellement haïr.

Challe carefully designates those qualities of character which offend his shipboard companions:

> Une taciturnité & une gravité inexprimable, . . . un esprit de primatie qui ne lui permet pas de se communiquer à personne, & un amour propre qui ne souffre aucun égal, & qui l'autorise à préferer son sentiment particulier à celui de tous les autres. . . . Tant pis pour lui: il faudra, . . . qu'il se réforme, ou qu'il se brouille avec tout le monde. (J I, 8–9)

However, in the course of a single battle at sea, Bouchetière was "reformed from a pompous fool to a worthy companion."[2] Challe's integrity requires that he attest to this change of character.

> La sincérité, dont j'ai toûjours fait profession, m'oblige de rendre justice à tout le monde. J'ai assez parlé de fois en termes méprisans du Chevalier de Bouchetiere; & c'est avec bien du plaisir pour moi, que je trouve l'occasion de lui rendre mon estime, & même très sincere, & très bien méritée. Je ne le croyois, ni brave, ni prévoyant. Je me trompais: il est certainement l'un & l'autre; & je puis assûrer comme témoin irréprochable & occulaire, qu'il a fait paroitre pendant l'action autant de sagesse que de bravoure. . . . Il ne se peut pas montrer plus de courage & plus de coeur. Tous les Officiers & tout l'Equipage en sont également charmez: aussi, n'en attendoit-on pas tant de lui. (J II, 98–99)

Challe's personal honesty and faith in man's capacity to improve, to develop and to attain his aspirations, inspired his words commending Bouchetière. To approach work, adventure, responsibility with an open mind and to judge with a sincere and honest attitude is characteristic of Challe. The

---

[2] Showalter, *Evolution of the French Novel*, p. 219, note 35.

term "sincere" appears frequently in his writings: he mentions his "plume sincére" with which he writes in the *Journal*, those "choses qui me paroissent très sérieuses." In these same introductory pages, he declares: "Je n'ai eu en vuë que la sincérité" (J I, 1–2). His purpose in compiling the *Journal* is presented in the light of sincerity and exactitude:

> Me proposant d'écrire tous les soirs ce qui sera arrivé dans la journée, on ne doit pas esperer de trouver un de ces stiles fleuris, qui rendent recommandables toutes sortes de Relations; mais on peut-être certain, qu'outre l'exactitude, la pure & simple verité s'y trouvera. Je suis naturellement sincére, & incapable d'imposer: ainsi, on poura croire avec assurance ce qu'on lira dans la suite; étant fortement résolu de donner pour mon compte un dementi au Proverbe vulgaire, qui dit, qu'il fait bon mentir à qui vient de loin. Je n'écrirai rien que je n'aie vû moi-même, ou du moins qui ne m'ait été assuré par des gens dignes de foi, & dont la fidélité ne me paroitra point suspecte. (J I, 12–13)

We have already cited numerous examples of Challe's respect for men of all beliefs and convictions. His travels brought him into contact with cultural and religious practices which strongly differed from European tradition. Challe penetrates the exterior manifestations of a given culture and divines the sincere human effort which directs certain customs or usages. During the stopover at the island of Moaly, the members of the fleet witnessed a prayer service in which the natives were "prosternez devant un squélette de Tête de Boeuf ou de Vache." Challe writes that his shipmates were both scandalized and amused by the scene.

> En effet, leurs éclats de rire furent si forts, que j'en étois confus. . . . Je fus peut-être le seul des Spectateurs qui prit les choses du bon côté. (J II, 63–64)

In Challian view, it is essential that the honest and sincere man be true to himself, develop his own talents, rely upon his own energies and industry for advancement. He reminds his readers that M. Hurtain is alone responsible for his advancement in maritime affairs, "n'ayant jamais eu d'autre Protecteur que lui-même."

> Le deffunt [M. Hurtain] par son merite personnel, & sa bravoure, avoit comme forcé la Fortune à lui rendre une partie de la justice qui lui étoit légitimement duë, & que la bassesse de sa naissance lui avoit deniée, en l'élevant de l'état le plus vil & le plus obscur de la Marine, dans un poste qui l'approchoit, & le faisoit participer au souverain Commandement; qu'il n'y étoit parvenu que par dégrez, & tous ces dégrez successifs, étoient autant de preuves convaincantes de son courage & de son application à remplir ses devoirs. (J I, 302)

Any form of patronage, all efforts to secure the support and patronage of the powerful, are severely criticized. Such usages are in contradiction to Challian ideals. The efforts of M. Ceberet to establish himself in the favor of the wealthy and powerful are noted:

> Je croi devoir dire, qu'il est Fils de feu Monsieur Ceberet Secretaire du Roi, l'un des premiers Interessez, dans la Compagnie de Guinée, qu'il a toûjours aimé la Marine, qu'il a fait plusieurs voyages de long-cours, & a épousé à la Martinique une Parente de Madame la Marquise de Maintenon. C'est un bel endroit pour ne manquer ni d'apui ni de Protection. (J I, 51)

In the Challian view of man, personal effort, honest endeavors, and qualities of character are the supreme test of his worth. Influential connections and other external ornamentation in no significant way add to a man's stature.

> Je croi pouvoir dire, qu'un Brevet de la Cour n'augmente, ni la bravoure, ni l'habilité de celui qui en est honnoré: pas plus que la Robe n'augmente la Droiture d'un Juge, ni un Bonnet la Science d'un Avocat. Cet Avocat reçoit le Bonnet quarré ce matin: en est-il plus sçavant qu'il n'étoit hier? Non: il est seulement mis en place de faire éclater sa Science; mais, s'il étoit ignorant, ce Bonnet ne détruit nullement son Ignorance. L'exterieur n'ote, ni n'ajoute, à l'intérieur. (J I, 397)

This passage strikingly resembles a section from "Du Mérite Personnel" in *Les Caractères:*

> Un homme à la cour, et souvent à la ville, qui a un long manteau de soie ou de drap de Hollande, une ceinture large et placée haut sur l'estomac, le soulier de maroquin, la calotte de même, d'un beau grain, un collet bien fait et bien empesé, les cheveux arrangés et le teint vermeil, qui avec cela se souvient de quelques distinctions métaphysiques, explique ce que c'est que la lumière de gloire, et sait précisément comment l'on voit Dieu, cela s'appelle un Docteur. Une personne humble, qui est ensevelie dans le cabinet, qui a médité, cherché, consulté, confronté, lu ou écrit pendant toute sa vie, est un homme docte. [3]

The man who lives simply, in accord with his position, activities, talents and training does not seek to draw attention

---

[3] La Bruyère, I, 160–61.

Challe's insistence that the criteria of a man's worth are not allied to the external manifestation of grandeur or rank, but dependent upon the individual's character and his contribution to his society is also reflected in the Salesian teaching on humility: "Nous appellons vaine la gloire qu'on se donne ou pour ce qui n'est pas en nous, ou pour ce qui est en nous mais non pas a nous, ou pour ce qui est en nous et a nous, mais qui ne mérite pas qu'on s'en glorifie. La noblesse de la race, la faveur des grands, l'honneur populaire, ce sont choses qui ne sont pas en nous, mais ou en nos predecesseurs, ou en l'estime d'autruy. Il y en a qui se rendent fiers et morgans pour estre sur un bon cheval, pour avoir un pennache en leur chapeau, pour estre habillés somptueusement; mais qui ne void cette folie? car s'il y a de la gloire pour cela, elle est pour le cheval, pour l'oyseau et pour le tailleur; et quelle lascheté de courage est ce d'emprunter son estime d'un cheval, d'une plume, d'un goderon? ... Les autres, pour un peu de science, veulent estre honorés et respectés du monde, comme si chacun devoit aller a l'escole chez eux et les tenir pour maistres: c'est pourquoy on les appelle pedans. Les autres se pavonnent sur la consideration de leur beauté, et croyent que tout le monde les muguette. Tout cela est extremement vain, sot et impertinent, et la gloire qu'on prend de si foibles subjetz s'appelle vaine, sotte et frivole. ... Ainsy, pour connoistre si un homme est vrayment sage, sçavant, genereux, noble, il faut voir si ses biens tendent a l'humilité, modestie et soumission, car alhors ce seront des vrays biens. ... La poursuite et l'amour de la vertu commence a nous rendre vertueux; mais la poursuite et amour des honneurs commence a nous rendre mesprisables et vituperables." St. François de Sales, *Introduction à la vie dévote*, 2 vols. (Paris: Fernand Roches, 1930), vol. I, 136–38.

to himself. He takes a legitimate pride in his own style of life; he fully respects the views and ways of life of others. This respect for others is not a passive quality; Challe believes that man is bound to undertake meaningful efforts to achieve understanding.

> Nous condamnons les actions de notre prochain, sans en connoître les motifs. "Homo considerat actus, Deus verò pensat intentiones,' dit a Kempis. Ne semble-t-il pas qu'il est de la Justice divine de nous mettre dans la même situation, & les mêmes circonstances, où notre Prochain s'est trouvé, pour connoitre par nous mêmes que nous avons témérairement condamné sa conduite, puisque nous faisons comme lui, & peut-être pis que lui, & nous rendre ainsi nos propres juges? (J I, 171)

This basic understanding of one's fellowman marks the ideal relationship between individuals. Challe encourages "complaisance sans bassesse" (J III, 54), the ability to coexist in a peaceful and cooperative climate with men of differing views. His words reflect the highest ideals of Christian community:

> Nous ne verrions point tant de perfidies ni de voracité, & très certainement l'Evangile seroit mieux suivi. Nous ne serions point à notre Prochain ce que nous ne voudrions pas qu'on nous fît. On n'entendroit point tant de medisances: on ne jugeroit pas si témérairement des actions de son Prochain; & nous regardant comme devant être tous les hommes ensemble, nous aurions pour chaque homme en particulier les mêmes égards que nous voudrions que tous les hommes en général eussent pour nous. (J I, 170)

An excessive attachment to power, reputation, or wealth destroys the integrity of an individual and weakens his *rapport* with others. Challe opens his third chapter of the *Mémoires* with a strong denunciation of those compatriots whose lives are dominated by a quest for wealth and other worldly riches:

> La probité et la droiture régnaient autrefois en France, et à présent il n'y en a plus. Les Français étaient autrefois

renommés pour leur bonne foi, ils sont à présent regardés d'un autre oeil. Cette vertu qui est le premier et le plus puissant lien de la société civile s'est perdu par degrés, à mesure que leurs chefs leur en ont montré l'exemple.... Je pose pour base de mon système que la bonne foi a disparu à mesure que l'avidité des richesses a augmenté et que chacun a voulu s'emparer des biens de son prochain. (M 31)

Wealth and social position do not necessarily reflect the innate qualities of a man. When considering the role of the Church as the servant of all men, Challe writes:

En effet, il est certain que le salut de l'ame d'un simple particulier est aussi précieux devant Dieu, que celui d'un gros Seigneur: tous deux sont égaux devant lui; c'est une vérité dont qui que ce soit ne doute. (J III, 39)

While Challian fictional heroes all have some employment for which they are responsible, none of them is seriously involved in the financial world. Since the practice of law is considered by Challe as a more honorable occupation, several of his fictional characters are lawyers (as was Challe himself): Jussy, Contamine and Des Prez are practicing lawyers; Des Prez' father is a judge; Des Ronais is affiliated with a judicial group. It will be recalled that Des Frans refuses to continue his work in the tax office: the avarice and insatiable greed of the tax collector and their oppression of the common people force him to seek other employment. Challe also devotes several pages of the *Mémoires* to the injustice commited against the common man in the name of taxation.

Il n'y avait que les ministres des Finances qui en fussent informés et ils se bouchaient eux-mêmes les yeux, les oreilles et le coeur, prenant toutes les précautions pour empêcher que les plaintes du peuple ne parvinssent jusqu'au prince. (M 42)

These injustices are all the more scandalous in view of the fortunes amassed by the collectors:

De là, sont venues aussi ces fortunes subites et éclatantes

> d'une infinité de coquins, qui ne méritent qu'on songe à eux, que pour les rendre odieux à la posterité.

Challe further describes these government representatives as

> scélérats tirés de la plus basse lie du peuple, qui ont presque tous su trouver, grâce à leurs richesses mal acquises, le moyen de s'asservir les gens de qualité, qui se sont avilis jusqu'à entrer dans leurs familles. (M 198)

The buying and selling of offices, the awarding of positions of prominence and power to the unqualified, are scandals which Challe brings to the attention of his readers. His concern is especially evident in those cases where places in the parliament are made available to the wealthy:

> Le Parlement, autrefois l'honneur du royaume, dont l'équité était si bien reconnue que les princes étrangers le prenaient pour juge ou pour arbitre de leurs différends, n'est plus à présent que l'ombre de ce qu'il a été, parce que les charges des membres qui le composent ne se donnent plus au mérite, mais seulement à ceux qui peuvent les acheter, qui, pour la plupart, se ressentent de la bassesse de leur origine, étant, du moins en grande partie, de race de maltôtiers, de partisans et autres, que la corruption du siècle a engendrés.... Je sais bien que nous avons parmi eux plusieurs magistrats d'ancienne extraction et même de bonne maison, mais je sais bien aussi qu'ils ne sont pas le plus grand nombre. Je sais bien encore qu'il y en a de très intègres et de très judicieux, mais je sais bien aussi qu'il y en a plusieurs fort peu scrupuleux et qui ne s'embarrassent pas de donner un soufflet au bon droit. Le malheur est qu'on ne pèse pas les voix, mais qu'on les compte. (M 36–37)

During the decades of war debt, the government was forced to initiate new means of revenue collection. "C'a été la création de charges qui ne sont qu'à charge au public." These posts were purchased by unqualified men motivated by greed for power and wealth. The common people bore the entire burden of the exemptions, privileges and dignities accorded to the rich.

L'argent devenant plus rare de jour en jour, il a fallu, pour en trouver, recourir à des moyens inconnus à nos pères.... On en [commission] a créé de toute espèce, et pour les faire acheter promptement, on leur a attribué des droits qui ont achevé de ruiner tout l'intérieur du royaume, et d'autres qui vont contre les commandements de Dieu, les droits de la nature et du sang et contre la charité chrétienne.

Les droits qui ont ruiné l'intérieur du royaume consistent en ce que les acquéreurs de ces charges étaient exempts de taille, de subsistances, de passage des gens de guerre, de sel et d'autres impositions que toute la communauté supportait. Les gros fermiers et les paysans riches ont acheté ces charges à cause des exemptions qui y étaient attachées, et comme il ne fallait pas que les revenus ordinaires fussent diminués, il a fallu augmenter les tailles et en faire supporter l'imposition aux pauvres, dont la quote-part a été si fort outrée, que les provinces en sont absolument ruinées, surtout le bas peuple. (M 19–20)

The reader should not conclude that Challe's interest in the average citizen is merely abstract or theoretical. On the contrary, he participates in the life of his colleagues; he fully shares the companionship and fellowship of his comrades. He describes himself as "un génie gay" (C 151. Letter dated December 30, 1713). His *joie de vivre* is particularly evident in the pages of the *Journal* in which he recounts leisure moments shared with friends aboard *L'Ecueil*, pleasantries exchanged and practical jokes performed. References to these shipboard gatherings and secret drinking bouts are described with enthusiasm and delight.

Nous faisons bonne chere, nous buvons de même, & il ne me paroit pas que personne s'embarasse du futur. En effet, 'sufficit diei malicia sua.' C'est profaner l'Ecriture Sainte, que de l'emploier ici; mais je n'y entens aucun mal: s'il faut jeuner, nous jeunerons; c'est tout. (J I, 79)

Challe prides himself on the simplicity of his life, the pleasure he finds in the unpretentious occupations of everyday living; discussions with his friends, writing the daily log of the journey to the Far East, quiet reading of his favorite authors.

Following a thorough study of Challe's views with regard to man's integration into his society, it becomes apparent that character should be considered the key to promotion and the assigning of positions. Positions of responsibility and leadership should never be awarded in return for favors received or with an intent to oblige. In describing the tone of the quasi-utopian colonies envisioned for the New World, Challe remarks:

> On devra également étudier le caractère et les talents de tous les membres de la colonie, afin de leur confier les emplois qui leur conviennent le mieux. Ces emplois, comme toutes les promotions, seront, après enquête, accordés par les bureaux de Paris, au mérite et jamais à la faveur. (M 259)

This same attitude is evident in his praise of the spirit which unites members of *Le Journal Littéraire de La Haye*:

> Ce que vous me dites de votre société me plait infiniment. Vous deviez adjouter qu'elle est réunie par la science et le vrai mérite. (C 163. Letter dated March 4, 1714.)

Challe's writings illustrate the theme of the goodness and perfectibility of human nature. Man's virtues outweigh his faults; his capabilities surpass his weaknesses. Basically good, man is capable of self-improvement. Challe illustrates this concept in several contexts, particularly in his references to M. Hurtain, the self-made man: "Imitons sa droiture, sa bonté, sa candeur, & sa foi" (J I, 307). The common man, or the average citizen, who forms the vast majority of the population of any nation, merits consideration and deserves the opportunity to develop fully his talents and abilities and to advance in society and in his post according to his qualities, training and experience. Since every member of society has a role to play in furthering the goals of that society, the citizen's virtues assume a singular significance in this social perspective. This appreciation of human virtue announces the definition formulated by Voltaire in the second half of the eighteenth century:

> Qu'est-ce que vertu? Bienfaisance envers le prochain. Puis-je appeler vertu autre chose que ce qui me fait du bien?
> N'admettra-t-on de vertus que celles qui sont utiles au prochain? Eh! comment puis-je en admettre d'autres? Nous vivons en société; il n'y a donc de véritablement bon pour nous que ce qui fait le bien de la société. . . . La vertu entre les hommes est un commerce de bienfaits. [4]

An earlier chapter of this study quotes Challe's denunciation of the political policies and economic programs which oppress the peasant, the working or common man; another chapter cites instances in which the Church and her representatives have not fully and selflessly dedicated themselves to the service of all men. The implications and the force of these criticisms become apparent through this study of the Challian appreciation of man, the vital contribution of each citizen to the welfare of his society.

---

[4] Voltaire, *Dictionnaire philosophique*, XX, 573–74.
This social awareness and respect for man, key themes in Challe's texts, is found in the writings of Diderot: "Et surtout être honnête et sincère jusqu'au scrupule avec des êtres fragiles qui ne peuvent faire notre bonheur, sans renoncer aux avantages les plus précieux de nos sociétés." *Supplément au voyage de Bougainville*, II, p. 249.

Chapter VI

Woman: Love and Marriage

For centuries ecclesiastical and civil tradition emphasized woman's subordinate role. Although the period studied by Challe, the second half of the seventeenth century and the early years of the eighteenth century, was not significantly exceptional, the literary and cultural influence exercised by such strong-minded women as Mme de Rambouillet, Mlle de Montpensier or Mme de Sully, should not be overlooked. The literary salons established and maintained by these figures played a dominant role in contemporary social circles. In principle, however, the seventeenth century spirit of absolutism led to a further subordination of woman:

> C'est qu'en réalité, le règne de Louis XIV est extrêmement défavorable à l'éclosion d'un mouvement féministe: car le triomphe de la monarchie absolue dans le domaine politique suppose, dans le domaine social, familial, religieux, moral, le triomphe d'autres conceptions, toutes hostiles à l'émancipation de la femme. ... Comme tout régime d'autorité, comme la Rome républicaine, comme la France de Napoléon, la monarchie absolue a pour substruction première une très forte organisation de la famille: l'autorité du père, héritier du 'pater familias,' doit, sur la femme comme sur les enfants, s'exercer sans restriction aucune.

Parler aux femmes d'émancipation, c'est les dresser contre leur maître légitime, contre celui qui dans la famillle représente le roi et Dieu. C'est porter l'anarchie au sein de la petite société qui est l'image de l'Etat. C'est par là même saper les bases. [1]

Much of this tradition persisted in the society of the eighteenth century. Socially, legally, woman remained a dependent; she was an eternal minor. Her activities, limited in scope, revolved in great measure around her pursuit of happiness.[2]

La femme n'est pas considérée comme un être libre, majeure, obligée de se faire par elle-même une place dans cette société et devant mettre, comme l'homme ses facultés, ses talents au service du bien public, mais comme une mineure éternelle qui ne saurait avoir pour son compte d'autres aspirations que le mariage ou le cloître, à qui la société ne réclame rien de plus de lui donner des enfants ou de prier pour elle. [3]

---

[1] Léon Abensour, "Introduction," *La Femme et le féminisme avant la révolution* (Paris: Léroux, 1923), XX.

[2] Edmond and Jules de Goncourt, *La Femme au dix-huitième siècle* (Paris: Charpentier, 1887), p. 514. "Cette philosophie que la femme se crée pour son besoin, aussi bien que pour son excuse, met son premier et son dernier mot, son but et sa fin, dans le bonheur."

[3] Abensour, pp. 457–58.
An eighteenth century critic describes discrimination against woman. The tone hints at long overdue change: "Le Sexe même entre en lice aujourd'hui avec les Auteurs Anciens & Modernes. Les mouches, le fard, la frisure, ne font pas l'étude de toutes les femmes, il en échappe toujours quelqu'une dans chaque Siécle, & dans celui-ci plus qu'en tout autre, qui se distingue autrement que par un ruban ou un bijou. Qu'on en conteroit de la sorte, si on leur donnoit une éducation, assortie à la vivacité de leur esprit, à la délicatesse de leurs sentimens? Mais soit jalousie, soit préjugé, on craint de leur ouvrir le Sanctuaire des Sciences. Est-il étonnant, après cela que l'esprit, qui veut être alimenté comme le corps, reste dans un état de foiblesse & de langueur. Il faut nécessairement que l'ame travaille; ou les vérités l'occupent, ou les chimeres. L'esprit des Femmes qui n'a point de ressource du côté de la science, se dédomage en se tournant du côté de la bagatelle, en retombant sur un évantail, sur un poupon. Il se repait nécessairement de caprices, de rapports, de chagrins, de minauderies. Mais est-ce leur faute, ou le défaut d'éducation?" M. Caraccioli, *Dialogue entre le siècle de Louis XIV et le siècle de Louis XV* (La Haye, 1751), pp. 105–06.

This is the society which Robert Challe recreates in *Les Illustres Françoises*. Aware of the social situation which confronts woman, he becomes her champion. He decries her dependence. "Few novelists made as clear a statement of the problem as did Challe in *Les Illustres Françoises*."[4] The seven tales which comprise this novel reflect the Parisian society of the 1670's; the plot is built upon the adventures of several young women who exemplify notable qualities of character. Readers familiar with Challe's nonfictional works may formulate the following question: Why should this adventurous and practical memorialist, dedicated to maritime and commercial affairs, turn to woman as the focal point of his single fictional work? A student at the *Collège de la Marche*, at an early age he began a vagabond existence, often at sea. It is quite normal that Challe should be totally at home with sailors, officers, merchants, and businessmen. To what, then, do we owe his interest in feminine psychology? Is it the result of that keen and penetrating gift of observation which marks his work? Whatever may be the source of Challe's inspiration, his women are vibrant individuals who confront the obstacles which hinder their pursuit of happiness. In many cases, they exhibit a tenacity of will and a purposefulness of surprising proportion. They are not male dominated: they are psychologically liberated, capable of initiating action. These young women evaluate situations, make decisions, act, and accept the consequences of their actions. At times they take a course of action which goes far beyond the accepted social or religious code of the day. The Challian heroine assumes a social role equal to that of her male counterpart; she is capable of assuming the rights and responsibilities of full citizenship.

These women are members of the bourgeoisie. They are not the *grandes dames* of high society, but *illustres* because of their notable qualities. Their stories are presented from a masculine perspective; the four narrators are men. Des Ronais describes the romance and marriage (two years previously) of

---

[4] Showalter, *Evolution of the French Novel*, p. 255.

Angélique and Contamine and his own broken engagement with Manon; Des Frans tells of the seven-year exile of Jussy followed by his recent wedding and the tragic and unexplained dénouement of his own marriage with Silvie; Terny recounts his successful scheme to marry Clémence; Dupuis restores a good name to Des Prez by revealing the circumstances surrounding the death of his wife, Madeleine, and concludes the series with the story of his own life.[5]

This use of masculine narrators in a work entitled *Les Illustres Françoises* might be questioned. A double advantage is apparent. Challe's intent is to extoll the virtues and other qualities of his female characters. His narrative style is event and action oriented. In the absence of direct self-analysis or self-searching, with little opportunity for self-revelation on the part of the heroines, a third person narration is necessary.[6] Through the prism of a third person, Challe adds a dimension of psychological penetration and credibility. As observers external to the central action, these narrators present accounts, valid because of their objectivity. Since they praise certain qualities of the heroines, they can also justifiably point out apparent weaknesses or acts of misconduct. There are instances when doubts or distrust are indicated. Des Frans, seemingly betrayed by his wife, has cause to question feminine loyalty and sincerity; Des Ronais, victim of a chance misunderstanding, suffers the anguish of uncertainty. Through the benefit of hindsight, narrators can also offer personal evaluations of a given character or of her conduct. This variation in perspective and the presentation of both positive and negative evaluation lend additional credibility and objectivity to their words. Secondly, Challe sees the possibility of enhancing feminine qualities by presenting them from the masculine

---

[5] A diagram of the narrative plan of *Les Illustres Françoises* is presented in Deloffre's text, *La Nouvelle en France à l'âge classique* (Paris: Didier, 1967), p. 89.

[6] There is no indication here of attention to the type of first person narration developed by Marivaux in *La Vie de Marianne*. In this novel the heroine is presented through the dual register of recounted event and subsequent judgment and self-analysis.

point of view. The male narrator can enthusiastically extoll the physical beauty of the women; he can recite a litany of their qualities; he can present each heroine as the perfect lover, virtuous, wise, and accomplished.

It has already been noted that the narrative style of *Les Illustres Françoises* is action oriented. So, too, are the letters composed by the heroines. Despite the literary tradition attached to the revelatory nature of epistolary exchanges, the letters included in *Les Illustres Françoises* serve a dramatic function in the tales. They are stimulants to action; they can be termed "events" or a "necessary and integral part of the plot."[7] These letters, a fusion of experience and narration, reflect the active, energetic nature of their writers. In woman's circumscribed world, letters were a strong and effective weapon, a means of inciting the hero to some particular action. For example, through a series of letters, Clémence enlists the aid of Terny in releasing her from the cloister.[8] A letter from Madeleine to Des Prez, which falls into the possession of M. Des Prez, sets the scene for the catastrophic dénouement. The misconstrued letter from Terny to Clémence is the direct cause of the broken engagement of Des Ronais and Manon. Among all the letters, one is distinctive in its confidential and confessional tone: Silvie's letter to Gallouïn, in which she voices her perplexity and reveals her innocence. This single letter is unique in the pages of *Les Illustres Françoises* because its writer reviews and attempts to analyze the past. She also reveals her state of mind at the time of writing, her remorse and shame, and the sorrow endured since the time of her alleged fault.

---

[7] Vivienne Mylne, *The Eighteenth-Century French Novel: Techniques of Illusion* (New York: Barnes and Noble, 1965), p. 150.

[8] There are five letters composed by Clémence. Two studies have been made of these letters, comparing them to the five letters which compose the text of *Les Lettres portugaises:* Eva-Maria Knapp-Tepperberg, "Robert Chasles und die *Lettres Portugaises:* Kritik eines Vergleichs," *Germanisch-Romanische Monatsschrift,* 19 (1969), 24–33; Giorgio Mirandole, "Robert Chasles e le 'Lettres Portugaises,' *Studi Francesi,* 9 (1965), 271–75. Clémence's letters in *Les Illustres Françoises* are found as follows: I, 138–40; 143–44; 150–51; 153–54; 159–62.

However, the major portion of the letters included in this novel is intimately tied to the events described or the activities undertaken by the principal characters.[9]

The context of these letters is realistic. Frequently the gentleman travels extensively: Terny goes to war and at a later time leaves Paris for Avignon; Clémence awaits his return and her release from the convent. Babet spends the seven years of Jussy's exile in Paris; Manon remains at home while Des Ronais travels for business reasons.

The setting of the tales is also realistic: Parisian society of the 1670's. Details related to city parks and streets, public buildings and private dwellings are incorporated in the text. Challe's choice of names for his heroines is dictated by the preferences of the times:

> un mot à dire, au sujet des noms dérivez de ceux de batême que j'ai donnez à mes héroïnes, tels que Manon, Babet, & d'autres. J'ai suivi en cela l'usage qu'on suivoit lorsque les choses que je raconte se sont passées, où l'on voyoit des filles de distinction & de qualité nommées comme je les nomme. (IF, Préface, I, LXIV) [10]

The names selected by Challe frequently reveal a dimen-

---

[9] Forno counts twenty-seven letters and *billets* in the novel. Most of these have a functional value: "Far from having a decorative or instructional element, as were the letters sprinkled throughout the baroque novel, and unlike the pseudo-documentary letter of the 'nouvelle historique,' the letters exchanged between heroes and heroines of the several tales of *Les Illustres Françoises* play a serious role by spurring on the action and influencing the outcome of events, as well as by revealing character." "The Fictional Letter in the Memoir Novel: Robert Challe's *Illustres Françoises*," *Studies on Voltaire and the Eighteenth Century*, 81 (1971), 152.

It should be noted that a statement made by Prof. Forno with regard to the frequency of the letters in this novel is incorrect. He writes: "Only one story, Jussy-Fenoüil, contains no letters at all." *Ibid.*, p. 151. The reader can disprove this statement: *Les Illustres Françoises*, I, 177 gives the text of a note from Babet to Jussy; pp. 192 and 195 refer to other letters written. It is true that each of the other tales also contains some type of letter or *billet*.

[10] Challe chooses French names for his characters: "en effet ce sont des François que je produis, & non pas des étrangers" (IF, Préface, I, LIX).

sion of character; they indicate a relationship between the qualities and the role of a given heroine. "Angélique" befits a poor and virtuous woman; "Babet" and "Silvie" convey undertones of the romanesque, of adventure and perhaps of uncertain lineage. Angélique is presented as an impoverished young woman who patiently cares for an ailing mother; Babet and Silvie are highly emotional women. Babet is an orphan, but Silvie's past remains enigmatic. The name "Marie-Madeleine de l'Epine" evokes the biblical Mary Magdalen's sorrow for her transgressions of the moral codes and the figure of the suffering Christ, crowned with thorns, expiating the sins of mankind. The death scene of this young woman reinforces the duality of symbol.[11]

Challe situates his heroines in relationships which are authentic in late seventeenth century society, but which demand the exercise of initiative and determination as well as virtues such as constancy and fidelity. They are endowed with qualities which make possible their eventual triumph, acceptance or other form of success. Heroines are presented in relation to other characters: the mother-daughter (future mother-in-law/daughter) or father-daughter relationship is delineated.

In his presentations of these relationships Challe suggests or implies the need for a *juste milieu*. He holds Mme de l'Epine accountable for her wild rage when she learned of her daughter's secret marriage. "Elle étoit dans une fureur enragée & vomissoit feu & flâme." She becomes a "mére denaturée" (IF I, 257 and 267). As the immediate cause of the tragic death of her daughter, she is proof of the danger inherent in unleashed and irrational passions. In an earlier passage in *Les Illustres Françoises*, Challe emphasizes parental responsibiity:

> les péres & méres étoient coupables de la mauvaise conduite

---

[11] L. Versini studies the significance of names in the eighteenth century fictional writing: "Onomastique romanesque du XVIIIe siècle," *Revue d'Histoire Littéraire de la France*, 61 (1961), 177–87.

de leurs enfans, lors qu'ils forçoient leur inclination, soit pour le mariage, soit pour le couvent. (IF I, 22)

Challe does not uphold a disregard of parental wishes. He prefers the establishment of a climate of understanding between parents and offspring. Young love constantly repudiated by parents is pitiful; youthful disregard of family and social obligations can lead to tragedy. Challe holds the view that children owe respect and obedience to their parents and have the obligation of caring for parents. Children have the right to transgress parental injunctions only when these prove to be unreasonable. The example of the compliance and almost servile obedience of Clémence is striking. She lived under "la tyrannie de son pére," and during her father's illness, she "s'abaissoit à des services indignes, non seulement d'une fille de naissance, mais même d'un domestique" (IF I, 22 and 131). A plan of rebellion is set in motion only after months of this intolerable situation. The efforts of the young couple to win permission to marry, their long sustained compliance with his wishes earn them eventual happiness.

This situation offers Challe the opportunity of expressing his views on forced religious vocations. The young Bernay tells his friend, Terny: "qu'il n'approuvoit point la tyrannie de son pére qui vouloit cloitrer une partie de ses enfans pour avantager les autres." The early pages of the tale reveal a strongly negative assessment of convent life. Terny refers to the life in terms of imprisonment; he finds it a "sacrilège tout pur" to so "séquestrer" a beautiful young girl (IF I, 130–31). Since such statements are unchallenged, they can be considered allied to the position of their author.

The Clémence-Terny tale is an intensification of the problem faced by Manon and Des Ronais vis-à-vis old Dupuis. Their repeated requests to marry go unheeded. In the end they must await the death of the old gentleman who insisted that his daughter's affections and interests remain undividedly his. Dupuis wished to be cared for by a loving daughter; he admitted

qu'il n'avoit retiré sa fille auprès de lui que pour en être

> soigné & soulagé sur la fin de sa vie, non pas pour la faire passer entre les bras d'un homme, qui pourroit l'empêcher femme, d'avoir pour lui les égards & l'attachement qu'elle avoit fille. (IF I, 19)

In his "Préface" Challe comments favorably on this view; he adheres to the principle of filial obedience in normal family situations:

> L'histoire de Des Ronais fait voir que si tous les péres & méres en agissoient à l'égard de leurs enfans, comme Dupuis en agit à l'égard de sa fille, ils en seroient toujours honorez & respectez, & qu'on ne verroit point dans la misére, des vieillards qui s'y sont mis en faveur d'enfans assez dénaturez pour se moquer d'eux, dans la jouïssance des biens dont ils se sont dépouillez en leur faveur. (IF, Préface, I, LIX-LX) [12]

Challe distinguishes, however, between normal situations and overly authoritarian poses on the part of parents. In the *Mémoires* Challe recounts the dire consequences of the parent-arranged marriage between the Count of Evreux and the young daughter of Antoine Crozat.[13] This misalliance bore nothing but unhappiness.

> Cependant, il [Evreux] ne l' [his wife] a considérée que comme un moyen assuré de tirer la substance de Crozat, qu'il a sucée et suce encore de toutes ses forces. ... De l'indifférence pour sa femme, il a passé jusqu'à la dureté, ayant fait murer une porte de communication, qui conduisait de son appartement à celui de Mme Crozat, sa mère, près de qui elle allait souvent déplorer le malheur de son

---

[12] This quotation is a forerunner of the theme developed at length by Honoré de Balzac over a century later in his novel *Le Père Goriot*.

[13] "Antoine Crozat, surnommé le *Riche*, qui devint marquis du Châtel, fils d'un banquier, capitoul de Toulouse, était né dans cette ville en 1655 et mourut à Paris le 7 juin 1738. ... Il maria sa fille au comte d'Evreux, qui l'appelait son 'lingot d'or' et acheta la charge de trésorier de l'Ordre" (M 234, note 1).

mariage et la mauvaise conduite, à son égard, du comte son époux. Ce dernier a pensé que cette consolation était encore trop pour elle et l'en a privée. (M 237)

Challe seeks a balance between exaggerated meddling of parents in the affairs of their children and flagrant disregard on the part of young lovers of any restraint imposed by family.

In addition to these family relationships, Challe structures realistic social settings in which his fictional heroines must act and react. In more than one instance the young women are confronted by the problem of inequality (social or financial) between the lovers. Babet's wealth far exceeds the resources of Jussy; the reverse situation pertains in the case of Angélique and Contamine. In the working out of these tales, the heroines exhibit determination and resourcefulness, patience and fidelity, grace and refinement. Angélique is received at the home of the Princess de Cologny, an "honneur que cette Princesse n'accordoit qu'à des gens d'une vertu reconnuë, & d'un mérite distingué" (IF I, 121).[14] Babet's behaviour exemplifies total fidelity. She awaits the return of Jussy from his seven-year exile; she secretly visits their son; she lives a quiet, retired life, declaring publicly that she will never marry. Upon the return of Jussy their union is confirmed by "un mariage légitime," witnessed by Des Frans, who, in turn, acclaims Babet's constancy as "un prodige dans le siécle" (IF I, 194–96).

It should be noted that Des Frans expresses a cynical attitude toward feminine fidelity: "Vous sçaurez quelque jour, . . . par quel endroit l'infidelité des femmes est si bien établie dans mon esprit, & vous m'avoüerez que ce n'est pas sans raison que je me déchaine contre leurs fourbes & leur peu de bonne foi." Somewhat later he declares: "Ce n'est point

---

[14] The Challian heroine must confront obstacles, both social and psychological. Roelens diagrams the varying degrees of intensity of the obstacles dramatized in the first six tales. He indicates that social inequality is operative in four of the tales, parental (paternal) opposition, in two other instances. "Le Jeu romanesque et ses règles dans *Les Illustres Françaises*," *Revue d'Histoire Littéraire de la France*, 70 (1970), 940.

Jussy que j'admire, ... un homme a toujours de la constance de reste; c'est elle qui est à admirer, ... car les femmes sont presque toutes des fourbes" (IF I, 196 and 203).

At the time of the recounting of the tales, Angélique has been married for two years. From this vantage point of success and security, she serves as the voice of the assembled members of the group. In a formal manner she pronounces the blessing of society on the fidelity of the young couple, Jussy-Babet:

> Je sçai bon gré à Madame de Jussy; sa constance fait que je lui pardonne volontiers sa faute; en effet elle l'a lavée, & n'en est à present que plus à estimer; quoiqu'on ne doive pas l'imiter. (IF I, 203)

In a less dramatic fashion, Manon Dupuis illustrates feminine fidelity. After months of separation from Des Ronais, following a misunderstanding, she speaks of the man she loves in these terms:

> Je l'ai toujours regardé comme mon mari: sur ce pié-là je pardonne à ses mauvaises humeurs, & veux en agir avec lui, comme si j'étois en effet sa femme; parce que je la serai quand il voudra. (IF I, 63)

A lengthy passage in the *Journal* describes Mme Martin who lived with her husband "dans une union parfaite, mais, dans une très grande nécessité de toutes choses." When her husband was offered a position with *La Compagnie d'Orient* and spent more than twenty years in the Far East, separated from his family, Mme Martin supported her children and herself by peddling fish. When M. Martin requested that he rejoin his family, the company decided to bring his wife and children to the Far East.

> Il y avoit vingt-deux ans & plus, qu'il étoit parti sans dire adieu à sa Femme, & sans lui dire où il alloit, en un mot, qu'il l'avoit abandonnée; & depuis ce tems, ils n'avoient eu aucune nouvelle l'un de l'autre.

Friends, who located the wife of M. Martin, were deeply moved by the devotion and fidelity of this woman:

> Elle ne leur repondait que les larmes aux yeux, ... elle apprit enfin avec une joye inexprimable la fortune de son Mari, & ce qu'il étoit, & la tendresse qu'il lui avoit conservée. (J III, 13–17)

In addition to the virtue of fidelity, the Challian heroine exhibits an intense sensitivity. Madeleine is the clearest illustration of this quality. There is an undercurrent of tragedy which runs from the opening sentence of the Madeleine-Des Prez tale to the catastrophic dénouement; Madeleine is plagued by premonitions of disaster. She summarizes her foreboding by these words addressed to Des Prez: "Car enfin, je ne voi aucune heureuse issüe ni pour vous, ni pour moi" (IF I, 216).

Tales one to four are essentially happy in tone. The opening sentence of the fifth tale, recounted by Dupuis reveals imminent catastrophe:

> Il y a environ deux ans, qu'au retour d'un voyage que j'avois été faire à la suite du Roi, pour quelques affaires que j'avois à la suite du Conseil, j'apris que Mademoiselle de l'Epine l'ainée étoit morte dans un état pitoyable il n'y avoit pas plus que de trois mois. (IF I, 207)

Madeleine invents a story, implying thereby her presentiment of doom:

> Elle ... ajouta qu'elle & moi [Des Prez] avions lû chez le libraire où sa mére nous avoit trouvez le matin, une histoire de deux amans, à qui leur amour avoit coûté la vie. Elle avoua que cela lui laissoit une idée très-cruelle. (IF I, 217)

This propensity for sensing imminent or threatening disaster places Madeleine on a plane somewhat removed from the other Challian heroines. She embodies many of the qualities of determination, devotion, constancy, and fidelity of such young women as Angélique, Manon, Clémence, or Babet. For example, Madeleine arranges the first secret meeting with Des Prez; she confesses her love for him at this first rendez-vous; she works out a means of exchanging letters. She is a composite of these heroines and a link to the heroine of the sixth story,

Silvie-Des Frans, whose love is also overshadowed by tragedy. Madeleine is more sensitive than Silvie. She is painfully aware of the fragility of the happiness enjoyed by Des Prez:

> Je ne sçai ce que vous deviendrez; mais pour ce qui me regarde, le coeur ne me prédit rien de bon de tout ce qui peut réüssir de vos poursuites; & si j'en croyois mes pressentimens, je vous ôterois toute espérance. (IF I, 214)

The spiritual side of Madeleine's character, introduced through her many premonitions, reinforced through the symbolism of her name and brought to its full flowering in her martyr's death, makes of her an *alter Christus*. Instead of self-pity, accusations, or blame of others, Madeleine exemplifies forgiveness of injuries and forgetfulness of self. She accepts her suffering and abandonment; she does not seek the solace of understanding. Her travail brings forth a renewed charity and Christian pardon.[15] Her death, in the midst of the outcasts of society, "dans la compagnie & au rang de cinquante mille gueuses, tristes rebuts de la débauche & des mauvais lieux de Paris" (IF I, 268), reflects an *Old Testament* passage:

> Oui, j'entends les cris comme d'une femme en travail,
> les affres comme d'une jeune accouchée;
> ce sont les cris de la fille de Sion qui geint et
> qui tend les mains;
> "Ah! malheur à moi! je succombe
> sous les coups des meurtriers." [16]

This Christ figure, stretched upon a "méchant lit," watched over by a sorrowful mother, speaks of universal and unconditional pardon: "Je ne m'infome point des auteurs de ma mort, parce que je veux pardonner à tout le monde" (IF I, 268).

Comparison of the Challian heroines lends further support to the idea that Madeleine enjoys a place apart. All

---

[15] As an *alter Christus*, Madeleine resembles the apostle Paul: "Mes petits enfants, vous que j'enfante à nouveau dans la douleur jusqu'à ce que le Christ soit formé en vous." "Epitre aux Galates," 4:19.

[16] "Jérémie," 4:31.

other heroines are "grandes, brunes, aux yeux noirs"; Madeleine, "grande et bien faite, les cheveux du plus beau blond qu'on puisse voir au monde . . . les yeux bleus" (IF I, 210).[17] This distinctive portrait affirms her sensitivity and her spiritual qualities, placing her above other Challian heroines.[18] Each young woman in the tales is endowed with dazzling beauty. Lovers or narrators describe the young heroines as follows: Des Prez' reaction to Madeleine: "Je fus ébloüi de sa beauté"; Jussy extolls Babet: "Vous voyez par son portrait que je suis excusable de l'avoir aimée, jusques au point de tout hazarder pour elle"; in speaking of Silvie, Des Frans says: "Il n'y avoit rien de plus beau que son corps." Clémence is "belle comme un ange"; Des Ronais is incapable of describing Manon: "Je n'entreprendrai point de vous faire son portrait, il est audessus de mes expressions." His is a love at first sight: "Je ne pus m'en défendre, je me livrai tout entier. J'avois conservé mon coeur jusques-là, je le rendis. Je l'aimai, ou plutôt je l'adorai dès le moment que je la vis. On ne dispose pas de son coeur comme on veut." According to Des Ronais, Angélique is "un racourci de ce que la Nature peut produire de plus beau & de plus accompli." Dupuis describes *La Veuve* in equally strong terms:

---

[17] This dichotomy of presentation is similar to, although not so developed as Honoré de Balzac's system of psycho-physiological character presentation. *La Comédie Humaine* presents passionate women, those ardent in their love and devotion, warm in human relationships, those who live and die devoted to the will of the man, as "brunes aux yeux noirs." In the Balzacian scheme, the blonde, blue-eyed heroine is frail, pale, idealistic and active, somewhat remote and, at times, cold. At the opposite end of the spectrum is the dark heroine, passionate, ardent and devoted. Pierre Abraham, "Couleur des Yeux" and "Couleur des Cheveux," *Recherches sur la création intellectuelle: créatures chez Balzac* (Paris: Gallimard, 1931).

[18] Lawrence Forno believes that Silvie is "unquestionably the most pathetic of Challe's heroines." "Challe's Portrayal of Women," *French Review*, 47, No. 5 (1974), 871. It is true that the sufferings of Silvie extend over a longer time period than those of Madeleine. Both heroines are abandoned; neither is apprised of all the factors of her situation. The manner in which Challe presents Madeleine would suggest that her role is an exalted one, and that she is intended to edify. Her loyalty, her quiet resignation, her charity can only be termed sublime.

> Une très belle femme, dont les cheveux . . . étoient aussi noirs que sa robe. Elle avoit le teint fort blanc & fort uni, la bouche la plus belle & la plus vermeille, que j'aye jamais vûë; les yeux à fleur de tête, noirs & pleins de feu & de vivacité. (IF II, 482)

Challe seeks to convince his readers of the invincible power of feminine beauty. Heroines profit from their beauty; they know how to gauge the effect of their demeanor. The ability to measure their effectiveness, to estimate the impression made by attitudes and poses and to turn each opportunity to some advantage, are talents carefully exploited by Angélique, in particular. She analyzes each turn of events:

> Elle de son côté, qui avoit remarqué dans ses yeux tout l'amour qu'il [Contamine] avoit pour elle, résolut de pousser sa fortune aussi loin qu'elle pourroit aller. Elle connoissoit qu'il étoit trop bien pris pour pouvoir se dégager & qu'avec le tems, elle l'améneroit au point de dire les grands mots: ainsi elle résolut de paroitre avec toute la vertu & la fierté qu'une fille peut avoir, sans pourtant le dégoûter par aucune incivilité. (IF I, 80)

Angélique continues these schemes over many months: "Elle joüit de son [Contamine's] trouble, de son impatience, & du triomphe de sa beauté" (IF I, 84). Following the death of her ailing mother, Angélique lives "fort sagement & fort retirée" (IF I, 100). She leaves her home only to visit the Church. This use of religion, of the formal practice of the cult, serves Angélique as a sort of outer cloak in much the same manner it will later serve Marivaux' Marianne. The famous church scene in the early pages of *La Vie de Marianne* is a development and an expansion of Angélique's strategy.[19]

---

[19] Angélique "ne sortoit jamais que pour aller à l'église ou se promener; & jamais seule; toujours avec les deux soeurs, & le plus souvent avec leur mére" (IF I, 100). Similarly, Marianne seeks to impress others by her appearance: "La place [in the church] que j'avais prise me mettait au milieu du monde dont je vous parle. Quelle fête! C'était la première fois que j'allais jouir un peu du

Such schemes are executed by young women, minors, who live under the authority of a parent or guardian. Each heroine, however, possesses strong self-determination. None consents, for instance, to become the mistress of her lover. Moved by respect for the Christian and social code, each insists on some marriage ceremony. Manon and Des Ronais request permission to marry at the bedside of the dying Dupuis. A dispensation from the archbishop of Paris is necessary for a marriage outside the Church. Meanwhile, Dupuis dies; the priest insists that "nous [Manon and Des Ronais] n'étions pas dans la situation de nous dispenser des cérémonies ordinaires de l'Eglise" (IF I, 54). There is no question here of a union outside of marriage. References to the marriage of Angélique and Contamine imply a Church service. The wedding was delayed by Contamine's illness; Angélique "ne suportoit qu'impatiëmment le retardement de la cérémonie. Ils furent enfin mariez, il y eut deux ans à Pâques" (IF I, 121). The marriage ceremony of Clémence and Terny is the most dramatic: their wedding vows replace the solemn vows in religion anticipated by the congregation. Des Frans requests and obtains a dispensation from wedding bans prior to his marriage with Silvie at the church of St. Paul at a midnight service.

At times the wedding ceremony is clandestine or private. Des Prez realizes that Madeleine "avoit trop de vertu pour [lui] rien accorder contre son devoir." Therefore, the couple request a secret, but sacramental marriage.

Nous ne demandons pas que notre marriage puisse paroître aux yeux des hommes puisque nous ne voulons pas même

---

mérite de ma petite figure.... A peine étais-je placée, que je fixai les yeux de tous les hommes." Marivaux, *La Vie de Marianne* (Paris: Classiques Garnier, 1963), p. 60.

Crocker summarizes Marianne's ability to scheme, to evaluate her effectiveness and to judge the reactions of others. Can not this description be applied with equal validity to a precursor of Marianne, the beautiful and determined Angélique? "She is very vain about her virtue, very self-conscious about it, and not a bit loth to put it to fruitful use in attaining her ends." *Age of Crisis: Man and World in Eighteenth Century French Thought* (Baltimore: Johns Hopkins Press, 1963), p. 418.

de certificat.... Si elle veut être effectivement mariée avec moi, je veux l'être effectivement avec elle; non seulement pour ma propre satisfaction & la tranquilité de ma conscience, mais aussi afin d'être retenu par le respect d'un véritable sacrement. (IF I, 230)

Madeleine and Des Prez agree that their marriage is essentially in accord with Church law:

> Excepté que les Loix du Prince n'étoient pas suivies pour la publication des bans, ni l'engistrement du mariage sur le livre de paroisse, le reste étoit conforme à la pratique ordinaire, & l'on ne pouvoit pas dire que notre mariage ne fût pas bon. (IF I, 240)

The case of Babet and Jussy is exceptional: a private contract. Babet requests that this contract be signed by Jussy and herself. The solemnity of her intention is proved by her fidelity to Jussy during the years of his exile and by the wedding ceremony performed upon his return to France.

> Nous nous fîmes chacun une promesse de mariage; & un morceau de papier nous tenant lieu de tout nous nous jurâmes une fidélité éternelle, & vécumes dès ce jour-là comme mari & femme. (IF I, 184) [20]

The consistency with which heroines approach the question of marriage, seeking a public or official recognition of their union, illustrates the Challian principle of adherence to moral or social norms.

The young women not only set the tone of their relationships with their lovers; they are directly involved in the plans; they undertake activities to overcome obstacles to their happiness. Babet is an amazing example of determined effort: ini-

---

[20] Roelens views this insistence on a marriage contract as illustrative of the virtue of the young women. "C'est la condition fondamentale de leur 'héroïsme', qui exclut donc toute solution romanesque comparable à celle que met en oeuvre l'abbé Prévost dans *Manon Lescaut*." "Le Jeu romanesque et ses règles," p. 941.

tially, she writes to Jussy, instructing him to break off his engagement with Mlle Grandet; she threatens suicide if Jussy does not accede to her wishes; finally, she urges that they run away together.[21] Jussy comments on Babet's determination:

> Elle ne goûta point mes raisons & voulut absolument que je l'enlevasse. Tout ce que je pus lui dire contre ce dessein ne la fit point changer. (IF I, 185–86)

With a similar tenacity of will, Clémence disobeys her father. By means of a clandestine correspondence with Terny, she accomplishes her end: escape from the convent and marriage with her lover. Silvie uses every available means, licit and otherwise, to prove herself worthy of the attention of Des Frans. She wields an extraordinary power over him. Challe makes frequent references to the magnetism of her hold on Des Frans and to the irresistible quality of her beauty and her presence. "Je [Des Frans] jettai les yeux sur elle dans ce moment; je me perdis" (IF II, 314). Believing her guilty of infidelity, Des Frans confines her to prison. He discovers that Silvie retains control of his emotions:

> Qu'elle étoit belle! Que j'en fus touché! Les larmes me vinrent aux yeux, elle me connoissoit trop, pour ne s'apercevoir pas du desordre où sa presence me mettoit. (IF II, 392)

These heroines are capable of publicly declaring their love; they willingly expose themselves to the public in order to win their happiness. Manon declares her love for Dupuis in the

---

[21] Jussy's desire to seek an alternative solution is based on several factors. He explains to Babet: "Qu'attendu sa jeunesse de près de dix années moins que moi, & la différence du bien & de la naissance, on ne manqueroit pas de m'accuser de subornation & de rapt. Que si nous étions arrêtez, le moins qu'il pouvoit lui en arriver, étoit d'être renfermée toute sa vie dans un couvent, & moi finir la mienne par la main d'un boureau. Que ce n'étoit pas un crime digne de mort que de faire des enfans; mais que le rapt en étoit un qui ne s'étoit jamais pardonné, surtout lors qu'il y avoit à présumer que, par le grand bien & la jeunesse de la fille & l'âge du garçon, il avoit agi par intérêt" (IF I, 185).

presence of another suitor, Dupont, and within the hearing of her lover:

> Elle rougit, mais ne balança pas un moment. Elle se jetta à genoux devant son pére sans regarder les Dupont; & je lui entendis dire en ma faveur tout ce qu'une fille sage, honnête, spirituelle & passionnée peut dire de plus fort. Elle finit par assurer son pére qu'elle ne feroit jamais rien de contraire à la vertu, & qui put lui déplaire; mais qu'elle le prioit de vouloir bien ne la point forcer en disposant d'elle malgré elle-même. (IF I, 37)

This scene prepares another of a more dramatic nature in which Babet pleads for the life of Jussy. The judge is ready to sentence the young man; Babet, seemingly strengthened by adversity,

> se jetta à genoux devant les juges: elle les suplia de lui rendre son mari; elle les assura que c'étoit elle qui m'avoit jetté dans l'état où j'étois, que je n'avois consenti à partir avec elle que lorsque je l'avois vuë résoluë à s'empoisonner; que je lui avois même arraché le poison des mains. Elle continua ses prieres à ma justification avec tant de larmes & tant de véhémence, que j'en fus attendri.

A sharp contrast is drawn by Challe between the reaction of Babet and of Jussy who describes himself in the following terms: "Je fus saisi au coeur, je tombai pamé; & je me vis sur un lit lors que je revins de ma pamoison" (IF I, 189).

Another, perhaps richer and fuller, perspective on the question of love and marriage is presented by a woman whose preëminence is marked by the strength of her words, by the assurance of her manner as well as by her privileged position in the lengthiest and last of the seven tales. She speaks in favor of enjoying life and of adapting oneself to its exigencies. Her identity is carefully guarded by her would-be-anonymous creator; she is known as *La Veuve*.

Convinced of man's penchant and determined quest for happiness, she says: "Je sçavois que chacun ne cherche uniquement que son plaisir dans le monde." For woman, the greatest happiness is found in love:

> En effet, y a-t-il au monde pour une femme d'autres plaisirs que ceux de l'amour? N'est-ce pas pour les goûter tranquillement sans traverse & avec honneur que nous nous résolvons d'accepter un maître en prenant un mari? & que nous nous abaissons jusqu'à n'avoir point d'autre volonté que la sienne, & à souffrir même ses mauvaises humeurs?

La Veuve explains that happiness lies in adapting oneself to the circumstances of life, according to one's conscience, to the customs, code, demands of society. This accommodation and adaptation require a self-mastery, a discipline, and a control of self:

> J'ai vécu, comme doit vivre une femme d'honneur avec son époux. J'ai suivi la coutume du païs où Dieu m'a fait naître, si j'avois pû m'en dispenser sans crainte ni scandale, je l'aurois fait; & c'est en cela que je fais consister la véritable vertu d'une femme, qui est de vaincre les passions où son penchant la porte.

It should be noted that *La Veuve* refuses to marry Dupuis. She assures him that they will love better and longer outside marriage: "nous nous aimerons mieux & plus long tems" (IF II, 477–99).[22] She believes that marriage prepares the way for

---

[22] The words of Contamine, after two years of marriage, indicate a certain validity in the view expressed by *La Veuve*. "Je veux dire que souvent la tendresse d'une femme est à charge à son époux: suivons toûjours mon exemple. Je rentre assez souvent au logis chargé d'affaires. J'y rêve, ma femme croit que je suis de mauvaise humeur, & vient, par des caresses hors de saison, me faire perdre une idée, que je ne ratrape plus. La même chose quand je suis à travailler dans mon cabinet. Je n'ose pas la faire retirer, crainte de lui donner du chagrin; de sorte que par consideration pour elle, & par celle qu'elle a pour moi, je passe assez souvent des momens, où je voudrois, sinon n'être pas marié, du moins être bien loin de ma femme: Ainsi il y a des chagrins dans le mariage, dont il n'y a qu'un mari qui puisse parler par experience, & puisque j'y en trouve, je suis persuadé que d'autres n'en manquent pas" (IF I, 278).

indifference, scorn, even hatred. Having endured an unhappy marriage, she speaks with the fulness of experience:

> Toute la famille à crû que j'étois la femme du monde la plus heureuse, & lui l'époux de Paris le plus fidele; & en effet, ni vous ni personne ne m'avez jamais entendu plaindre de son refroidissement pour moi, ni de ses débauches avec des coureuses. (IF II, 476)

La Veuve is not the only woman presented by Challe who must accept an unhappy situation and live without love. Mme de Mongey, née Grandet, was rejected by Jussy. Her family insisted upon her marriage with M. de Mongey,

> homme de qualité, campagnard & très-riche, qui commença par la voir, l'aimer, & la demander. Il étoit sans contredit un des plus désagréables & des plus malhonnêtes hommes du monde. Elle a souffert avec lui pendant plus de quatre ans tout ce qu'une femme de vertu peut souffrir d'un brutal, d'un jaloux, & d'un homme âgé. (IF I, 183)

Des Frans has asked this widow to marry him. Their marriage, based upon esteem, compatibility and experiences gained through past sufferings, promises happiness. Dupuis summarizes for both parties their honest and sincere compromise:

> Je ne me suis jamais senti pour elle ces empressemens vifs & cette ardeur qui ne part que d'une véritable simpatie tant requise dans les unions. . . . J'ai toujours eû pour elle une estime & une consideration toute extraordinaire, mais l'amour n'a point eû de part dans mes assiduitez auprès d'elle. (IF I, 274)

In the case of young lovers, Challe upholds the moral and social standards which require a restrained response to their love. Transgression of social norms (or secret marriages) can lead to unhappiness, as in the cases of Babet, Madeleine, and Silvie. However, Challe and his heroines believe that the rights of love demand consideration. In the instances in which the Challian heroine takes a course of action which goes beyond the accepted social code, her patience and tact, her beauty and virtue eventually earn social approval. In such instances, the merits of the individual outweigh the factors of social position. Through his presentation of these heroines, Challe indubitably becomes a champion of women. Each of the heroines in *Les Illustres Françoises* is a figure of prominence. She is distinctly drawn; she possesses fine qualities of character. As a free member of society, she is independent, resourceful, determined upon the course of action which will bring her happiness. At no time can she be considered dominated by her male counterpart; she is not naturally submissive. All of these young women are aware of their essential role as members of society; their freedom implies responsibility to that society. Viewed as a composite through the perspective of *Les Illustres Françoises*, these heroines truly embody vital aspects of Challian thought.

Conclusion

This presentation of the social views of Robert Challe draws upon both documentary and fictional writings: the *Mémoires*, the *Journal*, the *Correspondance*, and *Les Illustres Françoises*. In each of these texts one finds considerable data relevant to the social institutions of late seventeenth and early eighteenth century France, the political and ecclesiastical leaders, and the citizens served by these institutions and their representatives. Since Challe is both a loyal Frenchman, who supports the concept of the Divine Right of kings, and an orthodox Catholic, special emphasis has been placed on his evaluation and appreciation of the role of the two great institutions of his society: the monarchy and the Church.

A careful analyst, a keen observer and a man dedicated to truth, Challe outlines the problems which confront his society. His talent as social critic is developed through his personal observations and his varied experiences, his contact with court figures, members of the ministry, commercial and colonial colleagues, as well as members of several literary groups. An active and contributing member of the bourgeoisie, engaged in trade and colonization, Challe asserts that social institutions exist, not in their own right, but for the welfare of the people they serve. His criticism is both theoretical and practical. Challe's texts provide specific and frank assessment of prolonged warfare, famine, uncontrolled taxation; they attest to dangers in absolute power and authority. Challe endorses the principles of Christian government: integrity, justice, mercy, tolerance; he considers the purpose of government allied to the preservation of the liberties of the individual citizen and the development of the nation and the well-being of her citizens. Specifically, Challe envisions political leadership exercised by a wise, selfless, and informed ruler whose authority is clearly defined and who is accountable to God and to his subjects for his decisions and policies.

Equally strong and direct is Challe's criticism of ecclesiastical leaders whose activities contradict their professional commitment. Challe views the Church as the guardian and interpreter of revealed truth. He also believes that all members of the Church share the privilege and the responsibility to teach the Christian message. However, Challe's personal adherence to the Church does not conflict with the conviction which pervades his thinking and his writing: respect for man's freedom of conscience.

For some readers, Challe's social criticism may seem idealistic. At one point in the *Mémoires*, he observes: "Je sais bien que ceci n'est et ne sera regardé que comme une utopie" (M 256). His outlook is optimistic: human nature is good; man is perfectible; progress is a goal worth human endeavor; individuals, notwithstanding the differences which seemingly separate them, can achieve unity and confraternity. The basis of sound social relations is *la bonne foi*. Challe's ideal micro-society for colonial life fully exemplifies "l'esprit de société, qui réunit naturellement les hommes" (M 257). This plan is the culminating point of his social theory. Through the combined efforts of all members, a spirit of interdependence, mutual respect, and tolerance can be developed.

Many of the ideas explored, studied, and expressed by Challe prefigure trends of eighteenth century thought. His commitment to "l'utilité générale" will evolve into a Voltairian definition of virtue: "la bienfaisance"; concern with the abuses of absolute power announces Montesquieu's theory of the balance of political powers; his condemnation of the injustices endured by the common man will be reiterated and developed by the impassioned words of Rousseau.

A truly human spirit pervades the writings of Robert Challe. Aware of the frailty of man, conscious of the good and bad qualities which affect him, exposed to the deceptions and disappointments of life, Challe proclaims faith in living, gratitude to be alive, and willingness to adapt (and to compromise, when necessary) in order to meet the exigencies of human existence. In this respect, his ideas clearly bespeak the optimistic spirit of the evolving epoch of the Enlightenment.

Bibliography

I. Works by Robert Challe

[Challe, Robert]. *Journal d'un voyage fait aux Indes Orientales par une escadre de six vaisseaux commandez par Mr. Du Quesne, depuis le 24 février 1690, jusqu'au 20 août 1691, par ordre de la Compagnie des Indes Orientales.* 3 vols. Rouen: Jean-Batiste Machuel, 1721.

———. *Journal d'un voyage fait aux Indes*, eds. F. Deloffre et M. Menemencioglu. Paris: Mercure de France, 1979.

———."Lettres inédites" (1683), *Letterbook relating to Québec and other places in Canada*, pp. 45–50. [n.d.]

Challes, Robert. *Un Colonial au temps de Colbert: Mémoires de Robert Challes, écrivain du roi*, ed. A. Augustin-Thierry. Paris: Plon, 1931.

———. *Histoire de Monsieur Dupuis et de Mademoiselle de Londé*, ed. G. Pillement. 2 vols. Paris: La Connaissance, 1927.

———. *Voyage aux Indes d'une escadre française (1690–1691)*, ed. A. Augustin-Thierry. Paris: Plon, 1933.

[Chasles, Robert]. *Continuation de l'histoire de l'admirable Don Quichotte de La Manche.* tome VI. Lyon: Amaulry, 1723.

Chasles, Robert. *OEuvres complètes de Robert Chasles: Les Illustres Françoises*, ed. F. Deloffre. 2 vols. Paris: Belles Lettres, 1967.

———. *The Illustrious French Lovers; Being the True Histories of the Amours of Several French Persons of Quality. In which are contained a great Number of Excellent Examples, and rare and uncommon Accidents; Shewing the Polite Breeding and Gallantry of the Gentlemen and Ladies of the French Nation.* Written originally in French and translated into English by Mrs. P. Aubin. 2 vols. London: D. Midwinter and Co., 1739.

"Une Correspondance littéraire au début du XVIIIe siècle: Robert Challes et Le Journal Littéraire de La Haye (1713–1718)," ed. F. Deloffre. *Annales Universitatis Saraviensis*, Sarrbrücken: Université de la Sarre, 3 (1954), 144–82.

II. Works about Robert Challe

Armegaud, L. "En Marge du préromantisme," *Revue d'Histoire Littéraire de la France*, 46 (1939), 235–36.

Billy, André. "Robert Challes, précurseur de Balzac et de Stendhal," *Figaro Littéraire*, (9 janvier, 1960), 4.

Carpenter, Edgar B. *Some Aspects of the Novelistic Technique of Robert Challes: Les Illustres Françoises*. Madison: University of Wisconsin, 1974.

Champfleury, Jules. *Le Réalisme*. Paris: Michel Lévy Frères, 1857.

Coulet, Henri. *Le Roman jusqu'à la Révolution*. 2 vols. Paris: Armand Colin, 1967.

———. "Le Thème de la 'Madeleine repentie' chez Challe, Prévost et Diderot," *Saggi e richerche di letteratura francese*, XIV (1975), 287–304.

Deloffre, Frédéric. "Un Mode préstendhalien d'expression de la sensibilité à la fin du XVIIe siècle," *Cahiers de l'Association Internationale des Etudes Françaises*, 11 (1959), 9–32.

———. *La Nouvelle en France à l'âge classique*. Paris: Didier, 1967.

———. "Le Problème de l'illusion romanesque et le renouvellement des techniques narratives entre 1700 et 1715," *La Littérature Narrative d'Imagination*, Colloque de Strasbourg, 1959. Paris: Presses Universitaires de France, 1961, 115–133.

———. "A La Recherche de Robert Chasles auteur des *Illustres Françaises* (1659–17..)," *Revue des Sciences Humains*, 95 (1959), 233–54.

———. "Robert Challe, Témoin de son temps en 1716," *La Régence*. Paris: Armand Colin, 1970. pp. 83–97.

Dethier, Tatiana. "La Peinture de l'amour et le renversement des valeurs dans *Les Illustres Françoises*," *Etudes de Lettres*, IX (avril-juin 1976), 17–30.

Engel, Claire-Eliana. *Figures et aventures du XVIIIe siècle*. Paris: Editions "Je Sers," 1939. pp. 183–87.

———. *Le Véritable Abbé Prévost*. Monaco: Editions du Rocher, 1957.

Falvey, John. "Psychological Analysis and Moral Ambiguity in the Narrative Process of Chasles, Prévost and Marivaux," *Studies on Voltaire and the Eighteenth Century*, 94 (1972), 141–58.

Forno, Lawrence. "Challe's Portrayal of Women," *French Review*, XLVII (April 1974), 865–73.

———. "The Fictional Letter in the Memoir Novel: Robert Challe's *Illustres Françoises*," *Studies on Voltaire and the Eighteenth Century*, 81 (1971), 149–61.

———. "The Rebirth of a Novelist: Robert Challe in 1973," *French Review*, XLVI (May 1973), 1138–47.

———. "Robert Challe and the Eighteenth Century," *Studies on Voltaire and the Eighteenth Century*, 79 (1971), 163–75.

———. *Robert Challe: Intimations of the Enlightenment*. Rutherford: Fairleigh Dickinson, 1972.

Francillon, Roger. "Du Roman-il au roman-je ou la conquête de la lucidité dans *Les Illustres Françoises*," *Etudes de Lettres*, IX (avril-juin 1976), 1–16.

Garsault, Alain. "Une Source des *Illustres Françaises* dans Robert Chasles: La Fausse Clélie de Subligny," *XVIIe Siècle, Revue publiée par la Société d'Etudes du XVIIe Siècle*, 79 (1968), 57–66.

Gevrey, Françoise. "L'Intrigue et l'objet chez Challe," *Littératures*, XXII (1975), 31–41.

Grimm, Friedrich Melchior. *Correspondance littéraire, philosophique et critique par Grimm, Diderot, Raynal, Meister, Etc.* ed. M. Tourneux. 16 vols. Paris: Garnier Frères, 1877–1882.

Henriot, Emile. "Les *Mémoires* de Robert Challes," *Courrier Littéraire: XVIIe Siècle*. tome 2. Paris: Albin Michel, 1959. pp. 314–20.

Jones, Shirley. "Robert Chasles serait-il l'auteur de l'Histoire véritable de Monsieur du Prat et de Mademoiselle Angélique?" *Revue des Sciences Humaines*, XXXV (1970), 39–49.

Knapp-Tepperberg, Eva-Maria. "Deux cas d'adultère dans la littérature française de la première moitié du XVIIIe siècle," *Studies on Voltaire and the Eighteenth Century*, 88 (1972), 859–70.

———. "Introduction," *Robert Challes "Illustres Françoises": Erzählte Wirklichkeit in der französischen Frühaufläarung*. Heidelberg: Carl Winter Universitätsverlag, 1970. pp. 11–15.

———. "Robert Chasles und die *Lettres Portugaises*: Kritik eines Vergleichs," Germanisch-Romanische Monatsschrift, 19 (1969), 24–33.

Lafarge, Catherine. "The Emergence of the Bourgeoisie," *Yale French Studies*, 32 (1964), 40–49.

———. *Les Illustres Françaises de Robert Challes*. New Haven: Yale University, 1966.

Le Blant, Robert. "Les Etudes historiques sur la colonie française d'Acadie (1603–1713)," *Revue d'Histoire des Colonies*, XXXV (1948), 84–113.

Le Marquand, H. "Un Faux témoin du drame de La Hougue," *Revue Historique*, 172 (1933), 58–67.

Marchand, Prosper. *Dictionnaire historique, ou mémoires historiques et critiques*. 2 vols. La Haye: Pierre de Hondt, 1758.

Marivaux, Pierre de Chamblain de. *La Vie de Marianne ou les aventures de Madame la comtesse de XXX*, ed. F. Deloffre. Paris: Garnier, 1957. "Introduction," pp. v-lxxxii.

Mars, Francis-L. "Avec Casanova à la poursuite du *Militaire philosophe*. Une Conjecture raisonnée: Challe," *Casanova Gleanings*, XIX (1976), 11–14.

Mirandola, Giorgio. "Robert Chasles e le *Lettres Portugaises*," *Studi Francesi*, 9 (1965), 271–75.

Mylne, Vivienne. Review of L. Forno's *Robert Challe: Intimations of the Enlightenment* in *Modern Language Review*, 69 (Oct. 1974), 870.

Nöckler, Horst-Werner. "Zu Den Auffassungen über Gattenwahl Und Ehe in Der Französischen Und Englischen Literatur Des 18. Jahrhunderts," *Neue Beiträge zur Literatur de Aufklärung*. Berlin: Rötten and Loening, 1964. pp. 107–28; 348–60.

———. "Studien zu Robert Challes unter besonderer Berücksichtigung der Eheauffassung," *Wissenschaftliche Seitschrift der Humboldt-Universität zu Berlin*, 8 (1958–59), 262–66.

Piva, Franco. "I *Mémoires et Aventures* di Prévost e le *Illustres Françoises* di Challes. Concordanze e influenze," *Aevum*, L (1976), 436–511.

Pizzorusso, Arnaldo. "Challe, l'inganno e la confusione," *Paragone*, XXVII (1976), 49–74.

Preston, Ann Wendy. *Robert Challe as Moralist*. Austin: University of Texas, 1972.

Prévost, Antoine François, abbé. *Histoire du Chevalier des Grieux et de Manon Lescaut*, eds. F. Deloffre and R. Picard. Paris: Garnier, 1965. "Introduction," pp. iii-clxxvii.

Reboussin, Marcel. "Connaissez-vous Robert Chasles?" *French Review*, XXXIX (Dec. 1965), 337–45.
Roddier, Henri. "Robert Challes, Inspirateur de Richardson et de l'abbé Prévost," *Revue de Littérature Comparée*, 21 (1947), 5–38.
Roelens, M. "Le Jeu romanesque et ses règles dans *Les Illustres Françaises*," *Revue d'Histoire Littéraire de la France*, 70 (1970), 931–52.
Root, Tamara G. "Epicurean Philosophy and the Realism of *Les Illustres Françoises*," *French Review*, XLVII, no. 6 (spring 1974), 31–37.
———. *Les Illustres Françoises: Social Realism and Some Intellectual Traditions of the Seventeenth Century*. Urbana–Champaign: University of Illinois, 1970.
Rousset, Jean. "L'Emploi de la première personne chez Chasles et Marivaux," *Cahiers de l'Association Internationale des Etudes Françaises*, 19 (1967), 101–14.
———. *Narcisse romancier. Etude sur la première personne dans le roman*. Paris: Corti, 1973.
Russell, Sister Lois Ann. "Robert Challe: A Voice for Reform," *Eighteenth-Century Life*, 3, No. 4 (1977), 123–27.
———. "Robert Challe: A Seventeenth Century View of North America and Freedom," *Proceedings of the Fifth Symposium on French-American Studies* (in press).
Showalter, English, Jr. "Did Robert Challe write a Sequel to *Don Quixote*?" *Romanic Review*, LXII, no 4 (Dec. 1971), 270–82.
———. *The Evolution of the French Novel: 1641–1782*. Princeton: Princeton University Press, 1972.
———. "Un Extrait des 'Illustres Françoises' publié en 1714: 'L'Amour innocent persécuté,' " *Revue d'Histoire Littéraire de la France*, LXX (1970), 103–108.
———. "Robert Challe and Don Quixote," *French Review*, XLV (May 1972), 1136–44.
Sottas, Jules. *Histoire de la Compagnie Royale des Indes Orientales (1664–1719)*. Paris: Plon-Nourrit, 1905.
Swiderski, Marie Laure. "Challe et les femmes d'après son *Journal de Voyage*," *Revue de l'Université d'Ottawa*, XLIV, no. 2 (avril–juin 1974), 178–201.
———. "L'Image de la femme dans le roman au début du XVIIIe siècle: *Les Illustres Françaises* de Robert Challe," *Studies on Voltaire and the Eighteenth Century*, XC (1972), 1505–18.
Therio, Adrien. "*Les Illustres Françoises*," *La Revue de l'Université Laval*, XVII (Dec. 1962), 335–44.
Versini, L. *Laclos et la tradition, essai sur les sources et la technique des Liaisons dangereuses*. Paris: Klincksieck, 1968.
Waldberg, Max Freiherr von. *Der empfindsame Roman in Frankreich*. Strassburg: Karl J. Trubner, 1906.

III. General Historical Criticism

Abensour, Léon. *La Femme et le féminisme avant la Révolution*. Paris: E. Leroux, 1923.
Abraham, Pierre. *Recherches sur la création intellectuelle: Créatures chez Balzac*. Paris: Gallimard, 1931.

Abraham, Pierre et Roland Desné. *Manuel d'histoire littéraire de la France.* 3 vols. Paris: Editions Sociales, 1966–1969.
Adam, Antoine. *Histoire de la littérature française au XVIIe siècle.* 5 vols. Paris: Dormat, 1956.
Aquinas, Thomas. *On Kingship to the King of Cyprus,* trans. Gerald B. Phelan. Toronto: Pontifical Institute of Medieval Studies, 1949.
———. *The Political Ideas of St. Thomas Aquinas,* ed. Dina Bigongiari. New York: Hafner Classics, 1953.
Ashley, M. P. *Louis XIV and the Greatness of France.* London: English Universities Press, Ltd., 1946.
Atkinson, Geoffroy. *The Extraordinary Voyage in French Literature before 1700.* New York: Columbia University Press, 1920.
———. *The Extraordinary Voyage in French Literature from 1700 to 1720.* Paris: Champion, 1922.
———. *Les Relations de voyage du XVIIe siècle et l'évolution des idées.* Paris: Champion, 1927.
———. *The Sentimental Revolution: French Writers of 1690–1740,* ed. Abraham C. Keller. Seattle and London: University of Washington Press, 1965.
Balzac, Honoré de. *Le Père Goriot* dans *La Comédie Humaine.* Vol. II. Paris: Bibliothèque de la Pléiade, 1966.
Becker, Carl. *The Heavenly City of the Eighteenth-Century Philosophers.* New Haven: Yale University Press, 1932.
Bénichou, Paul. *Morales du Grand Siècle.* Paris: Gallimard, 1948.
Bonnefon, Paul. *La Société française du XVIIIe siècle.* Paris: Armand Colin, 1924.
Bridel, Louis. *La Femme et le droit.* Paris: F. Pichon, 1884.
Brancourt, Jean-Pierre. *Le Duc de Saint-Simon et la monarchie.* Paris: Cujas, 1971.
Brooks, Peter. *The Novel of Worldliness: Crébillon, Marivaux, Laclos, Stendhal.* Princeton: Princeton University Press, 1968.
Brunetière, Ferdinand. *Etudes sur le XVIIIe siècle.* Paris: Hachette, 1911.
Busson, Henri. *La Religion des classiques (1660–1685).* Paris: Presses Universitaires de France, 1948.
Calvet, J. *La Littérature religieuse de François de Sales à Fénelon.* Paris: J. de Gigard, 1938.
Camus, Jean. *The Spirit of St. Francis de Sales.* New York: Benziger Bros., 1910.
Caraccioli, L.A. de. *Dialogue entre le siècle de Louis XIV et le siècle de Louis XV.* La Haye, 1751.
Cazes, Albert. *Pierre Bayle.* Paris: Dujarric et Cie., 1905.
Chateaubriand, François. *Oeuvres complètes.* 5 vols. Paris: F. Didot Frères, 1843.
Chinard, Gilbert. *L'Amérique et le rêve exotique dans la littérature française au XVIIe et au XVIIIe siècle.* Paris: Hachette, 1913.
Church, William, ed. *The Greatness of Louis XIV, Myth or Reality.* Boston: D.C. Heath and Co., 1972.
Cole, Charles Woolsey. *French Mercantilism: 1683–1700.* New York: Octagon Books, Inc., 1971.
Corneille, Pierre. *Théâtre complet.* 3 vols. Paris: Garnier Frères, 1942.
Crocker, Lester. *An Age of Crisis: Man and World in Eighteenth Century French Thought.* Baltimore: Johns Hopkins Press, 1963.
Daniel-Rops, Henri. *The Church in the Eighteenth Century,* trans. John Warrington. New York: Dutton & Co., 1964.

———. *The Church in the Seventeenth Century,* trans. J. J. Buckingham. New York: Dutton & Co., 1963.
Decaux, Alain. *Histoire des Françaises.* 2 vols. Paris: Librairie Académique Perrin, 1972.
Delvolvé, Jean. *Religion, critique et philosophie positive chez Pierre Bayle.* Paris: Alcan, 1906.
Diderot, Denis. *OEuvres complètes,* ed. J. Assézat and M. Tourneux, 20 vols. Paris: Garnier Frères, 1875–77.
Duchet, Michèle. *Anthropologie et histoire au siècle des lumières.* Paris: François Maspero, 1971.
Duclos. *Bibliothèque des mémoires relatifs à l'histoire de France pendant le 18e siècle,* ed. M. F. Barrière. Paris: Didot Frères, 1881.
Ducros, Louis. *French Society in the Eighteenth Century.* London: G. Bell and Sons, 1926.
Du Fresne de Francheville, M. *Histoire de la compagnie des Indes avec les titres de ses concessions et privilèges dressée sur les pièces authenthiques.* Paris: De bure, 1746.
Etiemble, René. *Romanciers du 18e siècle.* Paris: Gallimard, 1960.
Fargher, Richard. *Life and Letters in France: the 18th Century.* New York: C. Scribner, 1970.
Farrère, Claude. *Jean-Baptiste Colbert.* Paris: Grasset, 1954.
Fauchery, Pierre. *La Destinée féminine dans le roman européen du dix-huitième siècle: 1713–1807. Essai de Gynécomythie romanesque.* Paris: Armand Colin, 1972.
Fénelon, François de Salignac de La Mothe. *Oeuvres complètes.* 27 vols. Paris: Gauthier Frères, 1830.
Fielding, Henry. *The History of Tom Jones, a foundling.* New York: The Century Co., 1906.
Gaiffe, Félix. *L'Envers du Grand Siècle.* Paris: Albin Michel, 1924.
Gaxotte, Pierre. *La France de Louis XIV.* Paris: Hachette, 1946.
———. *Le Siècle de Louis XV.* Paris: Arthème Fayard, 1933.
Giraud, Marcel. "Tendances humanitaires à la fin du règne de Louis XIV," *Revue Historique,* CCIX (1953), 217–37.
Godenne, René. "L'Association 'Nouvelle-Petit Roman' entre 1650 et 1750," *Cahiers de l'Association Internationale des Etudes Françaises,* 18 (1966), 67–68.
———. *Histoire de la nouvelle française aux 17e et 18e siècles.* Genève: Droz, 1970.
Goncourt, Edmond and Jules de. *La Femme au dix-huitième siècle.* Paris: Charpentier, 1887.
Gooch, G. P. *Louis XV, the Monarchy in Decline.* London: Longmans, 1962.
Goubert, Pierre. *Louis XIV et Vingt millions de Français.* Paris: Fayard, 1966.
Green, Frederick C. *French Novelists, Manners and Ideas: from the Renaissance to the Revolution.* New York: Appleton and Co., 1930.
———. "Further Evidence of Realism in the French Novel of the Eighteenth Century," *Modern Language Notes,* XL (1925), 257–70.
———. *La Peinture des moeurs de la Bonne Société dans le roman français de 1715 à 1761.* Paris: Presses Universitaires de France, 1924.
———. "Realism in the French Novel in the First Half of the Eighteenth Century," *Modern Language Notes,* XXXVIII (1923), 321–29.
Grimal, Pierre. *Histoire mondiale de la femme.* 4 vols. Paris: Nouvelle Librairie de France, 1966.
Griselle, Eugène. *Fénelon, études historiques.* Paris: Hachette, 1911.
Guilleragues. *Lettres portugaises.* Paris: Garnier Frères, 1962.

Hatton, Ragnhild, ed. *Louis XIV and Absolutism.* Columbus: Ohio State University Press, 1976.
———. ed. *Louis XIV and Europe.* Columbus: Ohio State University Press, 1976.
———. "Louis XIV: Recent Gains in Historical Knowledge," *Journal of Modern History,* XLV (1973), 277–91.
Halévy, Daniel. *Vauban, Builder of Fortresses.* New York: The Dial Press, 1925.
Havens, George. *The Age of Ideas, from Reaction to Revolution in Eighteenth Century France.* New York: Holt, Rinehart and Winston, 1955.
Hazard, Paul. *La Crise de la conscience européenne (1680–1715).* Paris: Boivin, 1935.
Hippeau, M. *Oeuvres Choisies de Saint-Evremond.* Paris: Didot Frères, 1852.
Janet, Paul. *Fénelon.* Paris: Hachette, 1892.
Jones, Silas Paul. *A List of French Prose Fiction from 1700 to 1750.* New York: W. W. Wilson Co., 1939.
Judge, H. G. "Church and State under Louis XIV," *History,* XLV (1960), 217–33.
Kempis, Thomas A. *L'Imitation de Jésus-Christ.* Montréal: Granger Frères, 1910.
Kibédi Varga, A. "La Désagrégation de l'idéal classique dans le roman français de la première moitié du XVIIIe siècle," *Studies on Voltaire and the Eighteenth Century,* XXVI (1963), 965–98.
———. "Pour une Définition de la Nouvelle à l'époque classique," *Cahiers de l'Association Internatinale des Etudes Françaises,* 18 (1966), 53–65.
Kunstler, Charles. *La Vie quotidienne sous Louis XV.* Paris: Hachette, 1953.
La Bruyère, Jean de. *Les Caractères* in *Les Grands écrivains de la France,* ed. A. Regnier. 3 vols. Paris: Hachette, 1865.
Laporte, Jean. *La Doctrine de Port-Royal.* 2 vols. Paris: Presses Universitaires de France, 1923.
Lavisse, Ernest. *Histoire de France des origines à la révolution.* Paris: Hachette, 1911.
LeBreton, André. *Le Roman au dix-huitième siècle.* Paris: Société française d'Imprimerie et de Livrairie, 1898.
Lecercle, Jean-Louis. *L'Amour de l'idéal au réel.* Paris: Bordas, 1971.
Lewis, W. H. *The Splendid Century.* New York: Doubleday and Co., 1957.
Lough, John. *An Introduction to Eighteenth century France.* London: Longman's Green and Co., Ltd., 1960.
———. *An Introduction to Seventeenth century France.* New York: David McKay Co., Inc., 1969.
Marivaux, Pierre de Chamblain de. *La Vie de Marianne.* Paris: Garnier Frères, 1963.
Mauzi, Robert. *L'Idée du bonheur dans la littérature et la pensée françaises au XVIIIe siècle.* Paris: Armand Colin, 1960.
May, Georges. *Le Dilemme du roman au XVIIIe siècle: Etude sur les rapports du roman et la critique (1715–1761).* Paris: Presses Universitaires de France, 1963.
———. "The Eighteenth Century," *Yale French Studies,* 32 (1964), 29–39.
———. "L'Histoire a-t-elle engendré le roman? Aspects français de la question au seuil du siècle des lumières," *Revue d'Histoire Littéraire de la France,* 55 (1955), 155–76.
Miel, Jan. *Pascal and Theology.* Baltimore: Johns Hopkins Press, 1969.

Montaigne, Michel Eyquem de. *Essais*, ed. A. Thibaudet. Paris: Bibliothèque de la Pléiade, 1937.
Montesquieu, Charles de Secondat, baron de. *Oeuvres complètes*, ed. A. Masson. 3 vols. Paris: Nagel, 1950.
Mylne, Vivienne. *The Eighteenth-century French Novel: Techniques of Illusion*. New York: Barnes and Noble, 1965.
Ogg, David. *Louis XIV*. London: Thornton Butterworth, Ltd., 1933.
Packard, Laurence B. *The Age of Louis XIV*. New York: H. Holt and Co., 1929.
Parkman, Francis. *The Jesuits in North America in the Seventeenth Century*. Boston: Little, Brown and Co., 1886.
Pascal, Blaise. *Oeuvres complètes*. Paris: Editions du Seuil, 1963.
Perkins, James Breck. *France under the Regency*. New York: Houghton Mifflin Co., 1920.
Perroy, Edouard, et al. *Histoire de la France*. 2 vols. Paris: Hachette, 1950.
Pomeau, René. *La Politique de Voltaire*. Paris: Armand Colin, 1963.
Prévost, Antoine François, abbé. *Manon Lescaut*. Paris: Garnier Frères, 1965.
Racine, Jean. *Théâtre complet*. Paris: Garnier Frères, 1960.
Ratner, Moses. *Theory and Criticism of the Novel in France from "L'Astrée" to 1750*. New York: DePalma Publishing Co., 1938.
Raymond, Marcel. *Fénelon*. Paris: Desclée de Brouwer, 1967.
La Régence: Centre aixois d'études et de recherches sur le dix-huitième siècle. Paris: Armand Colin, 1970.
Rex, Walter. *Essays on Pierre Bayle and Religious Controversy*. The Hague: M. Nijhoff, 1965.
Richardson, Samuel. *Clarisse; or, the History of a Young Lady*, ed. John A. Burrell. New York: Modern Library, 1950.
Roman et lumières au XVIIIe siècle. Centre d'études et de recherches marxistes: Société française d'études du XVIIIe siècle. Paris: Editions Sociales, 1970.
Rothkrug, Lionel. *Opposition to Louis XIV: The Political and Social Origins of the French Enlightenment*. Princeton: Princeton University Press, 1965.
Rousseau, Jean-Jacques. *Oeuvres complètes de Jean-Jacques Rousseau*, eds. B. Gagnebin and M. Raymond. 4 vols. Paris: Bibliothèque de la Pléiade, 1959.
Rule, John C., ed. *Louis XIV*. Englewood Cliffs: Prentice-Hall, Inc. 1974.
―――. *Louis XIV and the Craft of Kingship*. Columbus: Ohio State University Press, 1969.
Sainte-Beuve, Charles Augustin. *Causeries du Lundi*. 15 vols. Paris: Garnier Frères, 1856.
La Sainte Bible, traduite en français sous la direction de l'Ecole Biblique de Jérusalem. Paris: Editions du Cerf, 1961.
Saint-Evremond, Charles de Marquetel de Saint-Denis de. *Oeuvres en prose*. 4 vols. Paris: Didier, 1965.
Saint-Germain, Jacques. *La Vie quotidienne en France à la fin du Grand Siècle*. Paris: Hachette, 1965.
Saint-Simon, Louis de Bouvroy, duc de. *Mémoires*. 7 vols. Paris: Gallimard, 1952.
Sales, François de. *Introduction à la vie dévote*. 2 vols. Paris: Fernand Roches, 1930.
Sée, Henri. *Les Idées politiques en France au XVIIIe Siècle*. Paris: Hachette, 1920.
Sévigné, Madame de, (Marie de Rabutin-Chantal, Marquise de). *Lettres*. 3 vols., ed. Gerard-Gailly. Paris: Gallimard, 1960.

Shklar, Judith. *Men and Citizens: A Study of Rousseau's Social Theory.* Cambridge: Cambridge University Press, 1969.

Showalter, English Jr. "Eighteenth-century French Fiction," *Eighteenth-Century Studies*, V (Spring 1972), 467–79.

Sicard, Augustin. *L'Ancien clergé de France: Les évêques avant la Révolution.* Paris: Victor Lecoffre, 1912.

Solé, Jacques. *Bayle, polémiste.* Paris: R. Laffont, 1972.

Spalatin, K. *Saint-Evremond.* Zagreb: University of Zagreb, 1934.

Spink, M. J. S. "Chronologie et composition thématique dans les ouvrages à forme biographique et autobiographique au XVIIIe siècle," *Cahiers de l'Association Internationale des Etudes Françaises*, 19 (1967), 115–28.

Spitzer, Leo. "A Propos de *La Vie de Marianne*," *Romanic Review*, 44 (1953), 102–26.

Stewart, Philip. *Imitation and Illusion in the French Memoir-Novel, 1700–1750: The Art of Make-Believe.* New Haven: Yale University Press, 1969.

Treasure, Geoffrey. *Seventeenth Century France.* Doubleday and Co., Garden City, 1966.

Vauban, Sébastien Le Prestre de. *Projet d'une dîme royale, suivi de deux écrits financiers*, ed. E. Coornaert. Paris: F. Alcan, 1933.

Versini, L. "De Quelques noms de personnages dans le roman du XVIIIe siècle," *Revue d'Histoire Littéraire de la France*, 61 (1961), 176–87.

Voltaire (François-Marie Arouet, dit). *Oeuvres complètes de Voltaire*, ed. Louis Moland, 52 vols. Paris: Garnier Frères, 1877–82.

Watt, Ian. *The Rise of the Novel: Studies in Defoe, Richardson and Fielding.* London: Chatto and Windus, 1957.

Wolf, John B. *Louis XIV.* New York: Norton, 1968.

INDEX

Abensour, Léon, 123
Abraham, Pierre, 135n
Acadia
   Challe's program, 50–55, 58, 82, et passim
   French colonies, 4, 10–11, 12, 13, 46–50, 73
Admirable, L', 67
Aquinas, Thomas, St., 25 and n
Archives des Colonies, 10–11, 13, 49–50
Arnauld, Antoine, 88
Atkinson, Geoffroy, 60
Aubin, Penelope, 9n
Augustin, Thierry, A., 94, 99n
Augustine, St., 20, 92

Balzac, Honoré, 130n, 135n
Bayle, Pierre, 102n
Bergier, Clerbaud, 10, 11, 12, 49, 50
Bernard, St., 20, 44
Bignon, Jean Paul, 9n
Bouchetière, 111–12
Brancourt, Jean-Pierre, 29n

Canceau, 12, 14, 49, 53
Caraccioli, M., 123n
Carpenter, Edgar, 2n
Ceberet, 106, 109, 114

Challe, Robert
   Biographical data, 8, 10, 15–17 et passim
   Character description, 22–23, et passim
   Ecrivain du roi, 15 and n, 16–17, 21, 108–9
   Name (spelling), 8 and n
   Social critic, 18–22, et passim
   Writings,
      Anonymous, 8–9, 18
      Correspondance, 3n, 5, 9 and n, 144
      Illustres Françoises, Les, 1, 2 and n, 3n, 5, 7, 9 and n, 124–44, et passim
      Heroines:
         Angélique, 97, 125, 128, 131, 132, 133, 135, 136, and n, 137;
         Babet, 27, 127, and n, 128, 131, 132, 133, 135, 138, 139 and n, 140, 142; Clémence, 101, 125, 126 and n, 127, 129, 133, 135, 137, 139; Madeleine, 27, 125, 126, 128, 133, 134 and n, 135 and n, 137–38, 142; Manon, 97, 125, 126, 127, 129, 132, 133, 135, 137, 139–40;

Silvie, 125, 126, 128, 134, 135 and n, 137, 139, 142; La Veuve, 135–36, 140–42
Parents: 38, 97, 126, 128, 129, 133, 134, 136, 137
Suitors: Contamine, 97, 117, 125, 131, 136, 137, 141n; Des Frans, 7, 38–39, 117, 125, 131, 134, 135, 137, 139, 142; Des Prez, 117, 125, 126, 133, 134, 135, 137–38; Des Ronais, 117, 124–25, 126, 127, 129, 130, 132, 135, 137; Dupuis, 97, 102, 106, 125, 133, 135, 139–40, 141, 142; Galoüin, 102, 126; Jussy, 117, 125, 127, and n, 131, 132, 135, 138, 139 and n, 140; Terny, 42, 125, 126, 127, 129, 137, 139
Journal,
1979 edition, 3n, 8 and n, 17
1721 edition, 3n, 4 and n, 5, 7, 16, 17, 21, 60, 61, 65, 82, 113, 119, 144
Mémoires, 3n, 4 and n, 5, 7, 11–12, 17, 18, 21, 28, 29, 42–43, 46, 53, 56, 59, 60, 116–17, 144, 145
La Suite de Don Quichotte, 3n, 17
Les Tablettes Chronologiques, 17
Champfleury, Jules, 2n
Charmot, 60 and n, 61n
Chateaubriand, Francois, 86–87
Chedabouctou, 12, 13–15, 49, 51
Chinard, Gilbert, 71–73, 72n
Colbert, Jean-Baptiste, 16, 45, 47 and n, 48
Compagnie de Canada, 13
Compagnie d'Orient, 132
Compagnie de Guinée, 114
Compagnie des Indes, 107
Compagnie des Indes Orientales, 16, 47–48, 60n
Compagnie des pêches sédentaires de l'Acadie, 10, 12, 14, 60n
Corneille, Pierre, 91–92
Coulet, Henri, 2n
Crocker, Lester, 137n
Crozat, Antoine, 130 and n

Deloffre, Frédéric
Critic: 3n, 8 and n, 9, 10, 15n, 17, 23, 60n, 61n, 74, 94, 99n, 125n, 127n
Editor of Challe's writings: 3 and n, 8n
Diderot, Denis, 27n, 42n, 56n, 101, 103n, 121n
Duchet, Michèle, 64n

Ecueil, L', 15, 23, 60, 61, 64, 80, 83, 85, 106, 109, 110, 119
Edit de Nantes, Revocation of, 34, 44–46, 100
English missionaries in Canada, 110
Enlightenment, 1, 23, 57, 58, 103, 146
Evreux (comte d'), 130

Fénelon, François de Salignac de La Mothe, 32, 33, 41 and n, 93n, 105
Forno, Lawrence, 2n, 127n, 135n
Francillon, Roger, 8n
Frères de la Charité, 54, 97–98
Fresne de Francheville, Du, 48n
Frontenac (comte de), 75

Gallicanism, 81 and n, 100
Giraud, Marcel, 44 and n
Goncourt, Edmond and Jules de, 123 and n
Gooch, J.P., 44
Goubert, Pierre, 43, 46

Hartig, Irmgard, 63
Hatton, Ragnhild, 30
Henriot, Emile, 20–21, 46
Huguenots, 45
Hurtain (captain), 20, 83, 106, 110, 113–14, 120

Iroquois, 71, 73–75

Jansenism, 81, 93–94
Jeremiah, 134
Jesuits
in Canada: 12, 54, 98–100
in France: 35–36, 88, 98–100
Journal Littéraire de La Haye, 2n, 3, 8, 9n, 10, 17, 19, 33, 88, 120
Judge, H.G., 44

Kempis, Thomas a, 89 and n, 116

158

Knapp-Tepperberg, Eva-Maria, 126n

La Boulaye, Charles Duret de Chevry, de, 12, 14
La Bruyère, Jean de, 26–27 and n, 101–2, 115
La Chassée, de, 20, 83
Lafarge, Catherine, 2n, 93
La Hougue, Battle of, 67
Le Marquand, H., 60n
Lesser Antilles, 78
Lossky, Andrew, 26, 28
Louis XIV, 7, 10, 12, 18, 26, et passim
Luke, St., 91

Marchand, Prosper, 2n, 11, 22, 59, 99n
Marivaux, Pierre de, 2, 125n, 136 and n
Martin, M. et Mme, 132–33
Martinique, 114
Maurepas (comte de), 12
Mazarin, Jules, 15n
Mesnard, Jean, 8n
Mirandole, Giorgio, 126n
Moaly, 84, 105, 113
Montaigne, Michel de, 70n, 103 and n
Montesquieu, Charles de, 55–57, 64, 146
Mousnier, Roland, 37
Mylne, Vivienne, 126

Nymwegen, Peace of, 44

Parkman, Francis, 99n
Pascal, Blaise, 93–94
Paul, St., 25n, 89n, 77, 134n
Peter, St., 92
Philip-Harbert, 110–11
Philosophes, 4, 23, 55, 103
Pondichery, 61–62, 68–70, 76, 79
Pontchartrain (comte de), 12, 42–43
Porrières, de (captain), 110
Port-Louis, 21
Portugal, 59, 100

Prévost, Antoine François, 2
Prince, Le, 16

Quietism, 81

Racine, Jean, 30n
Regnard, Le, 14
Religieuses hospitali/eres, 54, 97–98
Richardson, Samuel, 2
Roddier, Henri, 94
Roelens, M., 131n, 138n
Rothkrug, Lionel, 29, 57
Rousseau, Jean-Jacques, 40, 146

Saint-Castain, de, 74
Sainte-Beuve, Charles Augustin, 47n
Saint-Evremond, Charles de Marquetel de, 15 and n
Saint-Simon (duc de), 29–30, 29n, 32, 33 and n
Saint-Yago, 21, 61, 76–77
Sales, François de, St., 89n, 115n
Seignelay (marquis de), 10, 11, 12, 15, 16, 17, 49–50, 105
Sévigné (marquise de), 30
Showalter, English, Jr., 2n, 103, 112, 124
Soboul, Albert, 63
Société des Gens de Lettres et d'Esprit, 11, 19, 89
Society of Jesus, See Jesuits.

Tourville (comte de), 67 and n
Treasure, Geoffrey, 99n

Utopian tradition, 5, 63, 71, 97, 145
Utrecht, Treaty of, 42, 48, 50

Vauban, Sébastien, 40–41 and n
Versailles, 30, 34, 76
Versini, L., 128n
Voltaire (François-Marie Arouet, dit), 31 and n, 34n, 41, 55, 64, 71n, 103 and n, 120–21, 145

Wolf, John B., 26

studia humanitatis

PUBLISHED VOLUMES

Louis Marcello La Favia, *Benvenuto Rambaldi da Imola: Dantista.* xii–188 pp. US $9.25.

John O'Connor, *Balzac's Soluble Fish.* xii–252 pp. US $14.25.

Carlos García, *La desordenada codicia,* edición crítica de Giulio Massano. xii–220 pp. US $11.50.

Everett W. Hesse, *Interpretando la Comedia.* xii–184 pp. US $10.00.

Lewis Kamm, *The Object in Zola's* Rougon-Macquart. xii–160 pp. US $9.25.

Ann Bugliani, *Women and the Feminine Principle in the Works of Paul Claudel.* xii–144 pp. US $9.25.

Charlotte Frankel Gerrard, *Montherlant and Suicide.* xvi–72 pp. US $5.00.

The Two Hesperias. Literary Studies in Honor of Joseph G. Fucilla. Edited by Americo Bugliani. xx–372 pp. US $30.00.

Jean J. Smoot, *A Comparison of Plays by John M. Synge and Federico García Lorca: The Poets and Time.* xiii–220 pp. US $13.00.

Laclos. Critical Approaches to Les Liaisons dangereuses. Ed. Lloyd R. Free. xii–300 pp. US $17.00.

Julia Conaway Bondanella, *Petrarch's Visions and their Renaissance Analogues*. xii–120 pp. US $7.00.

Vincenzo Tripodi, *Studi su Foscolo e Stern*. xii–216 pp. US $13.00.

Genaro J. Pérez, *Formalist Elements in the Novels of Juan Goytisolo*. xii–216 pp. US $12.50.

Sara Maria Adler, *Calvino: The Writer as Fablemaker*. xviii–164 pp. US $11.50.

Lope de Vega, *El amor enamorado*, critical edition of John B. Wooldridge, Jr. xvi–236 pp. US $13.00.

Nancy Dersofi, *Arcadia and the Stage: A Study of the Theater of Angelo Beolco (called Ruzante)*. xii–180 pp. US $10.00

John A. Frey, *The Aesthetics of the Rougon-Macquart*. xvi–356 pp. US $20.00.

Chester W. Obuchowski, *Mars on Trial: War as Seen by French Writers of the Twentieth Century*. xiv–320 pp. US $20.00.

Jeremy T. Medina, *Spanish Realism: Theory and Practice of a Concept in the Nineteenth Century*. xviii–374 pp. US $17.50.

Mauda Bregoli-Russo, *Boiardo Lirico*. viii–204 pp. US $11.00.

Robert H. Miller, ed. *Sir John Harington: A Supplie or Addicion to the Catalogue of Bishops to the Yeare 1608*. xii–214 pp. US $13.50.

Nicolás E. Álvarez, *La obra literaria de Jorge Mañach*. vii–279 pp. US $14.50.

Mario Aste, *La narrativa di Luigi Pirandello: Dalle novelle al romanzo Uno, Nessuno, e Centomila*. xvi–200 pp. US $11.00.

Romance Literary Studies: Homage to Harvey L. Johnson, ed. Marie A. Wellington and Martha O'Nan. xxxvii–185 pp. US $15.00.

Mechthild Cranston, *Orion Resurgent: René Char, Poet of Presence*. xxiv–376 pp. US $22.50.

Frank A. Domínguez, *The Medieval Argonautica*. viii–122 pp. US $8.50.

Antonio Planells, *Cortázar: Metafísica y erotismo*. xvi–220 pp. US $10.50.

Lois Ann Russell, *Robert Challe: A Utopian Voice in the Early Enlightenment*. xiii–164 pp. US $12.50.

FORTHCOMING PUBLICATIONS

El cancionero del Bachiller Jhoan López, edición crítica de Rosalind Gabin.

Studies in Honor of Gerald E. Wade, edited by Sylvia Bowman, Bruno M. Damiani, Janet W. Díaz, E. Michael Gerli, Everett Hesse, John E. Keller, Luis Leal and Russell Sebold.

Helmut Hatzfeld, *Essais sur la littérature flamboyante*.

Joseph Barbarino, *The Latin Intervocalic Stops: A Quantitative and Comparative Study*.

Nancy D'Antuono, *Boccaccio's novelle in Lope's theatre*.

Novelistas femeninas de la postguerra española, ed. Janet W. Díaz.

La Discontenta and La Pythia, edition with introduction and notes by Nicholas A. De Mara.

Pero López de Ayala, *Crónica del Rey Don Pedro I*, edición crítica de Heanon y Constance Wilkins.

Albert H. Le May, *The Experimental Verse Theater of Valle-Inclán*.

Maria Elisa Ciavarelli, *La fuerza de la sangre en la literatura del Siglo de Oro*.

MARY LEE BRETZ, *La evolución novelística de Pío Baroja*.

DENNIS M. KRATZ, *Mocking Epic*.

CALDERÓN DE LA BARCA, *The Prodigal Magician*, translated and edited by Bruce W. Wardropper.

GEORGE E. MCSPADDEN, *Don Quixote and the Spanish Prologues*, volume I.

EVERETT HESSE, *New Perspectives on Comedia Criticism*.

ANTHONY A. CICCONE, *The Comedy of Language: Four Farces by Molière*.